u·x·l newsmakers

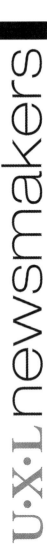

volume  two

Fi–McC

Judy Galens,
Kelle S. Sisung

Carol Brennan, *Contributing Writer*

Jennifer York Stock, *Project Editor*

U·X·L
An imprint of Thomson Gale,
a part of The Thomson Corporation

THOMSON
—★—™
GALE

Detroit • New York • San Francisco • San Diego • New Haven, Conn. • Waterville, Maine • London • Munich

U•X•L Newsmakers

Judy Galens, Kelle S. Sisung, and Carol Brennan

Project Editor
Jennifer York Stock

Editorial
Michael D. Lesniak, Allison McNeill

Rights Acquisition and Management
Peggie Ashlevitz, Edna Hedblad, Sue Rudolph

Imaging and Multimedia
Lezlie Light, Mike Logusz, Denay Wilding

Product Design
Kate Scheible

Composition
Evi Seoud

Manufacturing
Rita Wimberly

© 2005 Thomson Gale, a part of the Thomson Corporation.

Thomson and Star Logo are trademarks and Gale and UXL are registered trademarks used herein under license.

For more information, contact
Thomson Gale
27500 Drake Rd.
Farmington Hills, MI 48331-3535
Or you can visit our Internet site at
http://www.gale.com

ALL RIGHTS RESERVED
No part of this work covered by the copyright hereon may be reproduced or used in any form or by any means—graphic, electronic, or mechanical, including photocopying, recording, tap-ing, Web distribution, or information storage retrieval systems—without the written permission of the publisher.

For permission to use material from this product, submit your request via Web at http://www.gale-edit.com/per-missions, or you may download our Permissions Request form and submit your request by fax or mail to:

Permissions Department
Thomson Gale
27500 Drake Rd.
Farmington Hills, MI 48331-3535
Permissions Hotline:
248-699-8006 or 800-877-4253, ext. 8006
Fax: 248-699-8074 or 800-762-4058

Since this page cannot legibly accommodate all copyright notices, the acknowledgments constitute an extension of the copyright notice.

While every effort has been made to ensure the reliability of the information presented in this publication, Thomson Gale does not guarantee the accuracy of the data contained herein. Thomson Gale accepts no payment for listing; and inclusion in the publication of any organization, agency, institution, publication, service, or individual does not imply endorsement of the editors or publisher. Errors brought to the attention of the publisher and verified to the satisfaction of the publisher will be corrected in future editions.

LIBRARY OF CONGRESS CATALOGING-IN-PUBLICATION DATA

Galens, Judy, 1968-

UXL newsmakers / Judy Galens and Kelle S. Sisung ; Allison McNeill, project editor.

   p. cm.

Includes bibliographical references and index.

ISBN 0-7876-9189-5 (set) — ISBN 0-7876-9190-9 (v. 1)—ISBN 0-7876-9191-7 (v. 2)—ISBN 0-7876-9194-1 (v. 3)—ISBN 0-7876-9195-X (v. 4)

   1. Biography—20th century—Dictionaries, Juvenile. 2. Biography—21st century—Dictionaries, Juvenile. 3. Celebrities—Biography—Dictionaries, Juvenile. I. Sisung, Kelle S. II. McNeill, Allison. III. Title.

CT120.G26 2004
920'.009'051—dc22

           2004009426

Printed in the United States of America
10 9 8 7 6 5 4 3 2 1

contents

 contents

 volume **2** two

 volume **3** three

Italic type *indicates volume number.*

Entertainment

Government

Music

Science

Social Issues

Sports

Writing

U·*X*·*L Newsmakers* is the place to turn for information on personalities active on the current scene. Containing one hundred biographies, *U*·*X*·*L Newsmakers* covers contemporary figures who are making headlines in a variety of fields, including entertainment, government, literature, music, pop culture, science, and sports. Subjects include international figures, as well as people of diverse ethnic backgrounds.

Format

Biographies are arranged alphabetically across four volumes. Each entry opens with the individual's birth date, place of birth, and field of endeavor. Entries provide readers with information on the early life, influences, and career of the individual or group being profiled. Most entries feature one or more photographs of the subject, and all entries provide a list of sources for further reading about the individual or group. Readers may also locate entries by using the Field of Endeavor table of contents listed in the front of each volume, which lists biographees by vocation.

Features

- A Field of Endeavor table of contents, found at the front of each volume, allows readers to access the biographees by the category for which they are best known. Categories include: Art/Design, Business, Entertainment, Government, Music, Science, Social Issues, Sports, and Writing. When applicable, subjects are listed under more than one category for even greater access.

- Sidebars include information relating to the biographee's career and activities (for example, writings, awards, life milestones), brief biographies of related individuals, and explanations of movements, groups, and more, connected with the person.

- Quotes from and about the biographee offer insight into their lives and personal philosophies.

- More than 180 black-and-white photographs are featured across the volumes.

- Sources for further reading, including books, magazine articles, and Web sites, are provided at the end of each entry.

- A general index, found at the back of each volume, quickly points readers to the people and subjects discussed in *U•X•L Newsmakers*.

Comments and Suggestions

The individuals chosen for these volumes were drawn from all walks of life and from across a variety of professions. Many names came directly from the headlines of the day, while others were selected with the interests of students in mind. By no means is the list exhaustive. We welcome your suggestions for subjects to be profiled in future volumes of *U•X•L Newsmakers* as well as comments on this work itself. Please write: Editor, *U•X•L Newsmakers*, U•X•L, 27500 Drake Road, Farmington Hills, Michigan 48331-3535; call toll-free: 1-800-877-4253; or send an e-mail via www.gale.com.

U·X·L newsmakers

50 Cent

AP/Wide World Photos. Reproduced by permission.

July 6, 1976 • *Queens, New York*

Rap musician

The rapper known as 50 Cent is living proof that hip-hop is as much a lifestyle as it is a type of music. He was a star in the underground mix-tape circuit for several years, but the rest of the world did not hear about him until 2002, when his first single, "Wanksta," appeared on the soundtrack of the film *8 Mile*. In 2003, 50 Cent's debut album *Get Rich or Die Tryin'*, topped the charts and broke sales records. As a result, the young rapper was constantly in the press, and his life became an open book. This was not a "studio gangsta," meaning a musician who makes up stories about drugs, violence, and murder in order to sell records; 50 Cent was the real deal. He grew up on the streets of New York, survived being shot at nine times, and used those experiences to fuel his songs. As a result, critics noted that his music had a gritty edge, and they predicted that 50 Cent would be the next hip-hop heavyweight.

Life of a drug dealer

Born Curtis Jackson, 50 Cent grew up in South Jamaica, a neighborhood of Queens, which is a borough of New York City. It is a tough neighborhood, plagued by gang violence; it is also the birthplace of many rappers, including LL Cool J (1968–) and the female trio Salt N' Pepa. Fifty Cent was surrounded by violence from the day he was born. His mother, Sabrina Jackson, was only fifteen years old when he was born on July 6, 1976. She turned to dealing drugs in order to support her son, and eventually became one of the most feared drug dealers in Queens. Sabrina was killed mysteriously when her son was eight, perhaps the result of a drug war.

> "The bottom line is, the obstacles that you overcome are going to determine how great you are."

Fifty Cent was raised by his grandmother, whom he adored. However, because she had nine other children in her charge, the boy spent a good deal of time on the streets. By the time he was twelve, he was dealing crack, a strong form of cocaine that is smoked. As 50 Cent explained to Allison Samuels of *Newsweek,* he had to fend for himself because he did not want to burden his grandmother: "I didn't want to ask her for a pair of Air Jordans when I knew she couldn't afford them, so I began working to get my stuff and not stress her out."

At age fifteen, 50 Cent bought his first gun, and by nineteen years old he was the neighborhood drug kingpin, bringing in about $150,000 a month. He had dropped out of high school and was spending most of his time in jail; 50 Cent was also listening to his favorite musicians, including KRS-1, Rakim, and Run-DMC, and trying his hand at writing his own rhymes. He dreamed about breaking into the music business but was not sure he should give it a try. When his son, Marquise, was born, 50 Cent knew it was time to make a change: he decided to stop dealing drugs and start making music.

Eminem: Unlikely Hip-Hop Hero

Eminem is one of the biggest superstars in the music business, but he is also one of the most controversial. His lyrics are full of profanity; his CDs are boycotted by women's organizations and gay and lesbian groups; and he makes news headlines because of his public rampages against his mother, his ex-wife, other musicians, and fans. On the other hand, Eminem, a white rapper from Detroit, Michigan, has an enormous number of steadfast followers. He also has been credited with infusing new life into a genre that some considered to be growing old and stale.

Eminem was born Marshall Mathers III in Kansas City, Missouri, on October 17, 1972. When he was young, he and his mother, Debbie Mathers-Briggs, divided their time between Missouri and Detroit, Michigan. When he was twelve, the family finally put down roots in the east side of Detroit. Because they were constantly moving, Mathers found it difficult to make friends, so he turned to television and comic books. He also started tuning in to rap music, and soon he was writing rhymes like his favorite musicians, LL Cool J and 2 Live Crew. By high school, Mathers was skipping most of his classes, and focusing his energies on his music. He failed the ninth grade, and ended up dropping out of Osbourne High School.

Mathers paid his dues over the next few years, releasing independent CDs until he was noticed by veteran rapper Dr. Dre. With Dr. Dre's help, the world was introduced to Marshall Mathers, also known as Eminem, also known as *Slim Shady,* the title of his 1998 debut CD. His songs were harsh, filled with references to rape, violence, and drug use. In particular, Mathers lashed out at his ex-wife, Kim, and his mother, whom he blamed for his hard childhood. Critics loved him or hated him, parents protested, but millions of people bought his music and attended his concerts.

The *Slim Shady* CD was followed by *The Marshall Mathers LP* (2000) and *The Eminem Show* (2002). Both sold millions of copies and earned several Grammy Awards. In 2003 *The Eminem Show* won the Grammy for Best Rap Album. That same year Mathers took home an Academy Award for Best Original Song for "Lose Yourself," which appeared on the soundtrack of the movie *8 Mile* (2002). Mathers also starred in the film, playing Jimmy Smith, a would-be rapper who battles the streets of Detroit. Smith was a character that Eminem knew well since he moved from those same streets to become one of the most unlikely hip-hop heroes in music history.

Learns from the master

In 1996 a friend of 50 Cent's introduced him to one of his boyhood idols, Jam Master Jay (1965–2002), a member of the pioneer rap group Run-DMC. Jay was from the same neighborhood, and he saw a spark in the fledgling rapper. Soon, 50 Cent was studying with the seasoned musician. "He was really patient with me," 50 Cent told Josh Tyrangiel of *Time*. "I would come in with rhymes, almost free verse, and he explained that they had to fit 16 bars of music. Once he said it, I got it."

In 1997 Jam Master Jay signed a production deal with 50 Cent and agreed to promote him. The songs 50 Cent produced were raw, and his lyrics were taken from his own life on the streets. As Evan Serpick of *Entertainment Weekly* wrote, "they reverberated with authenticity."

Fifty Cent quickly became a hit in the underground world of hip-hop. This means he was recording and releasing discs independent of any major record company. As a result, the big record labels started to take notice of the "street thug"-turned rapper. In 1999 Columbia Records signed a deal with 50 Cent and gave him a reported $65,000 advance. Jam Master Jay received $50,000, and lawyers took the rest, so, even though he was a bona fide musician with a record deal, 50 Cent had no money. He kept his "day job," which meant that he continued to sell drugs to make ends meet.

Once they had 50 Cent under contract, Columbia was not sure what to do with him. Tired of waiting to release his first legitimate CD, 50 Cent cut his own single called "How to Rob." The song was an attempt to get noticed by his label. As 50 Cent told Serpick, "I needed them to stop and look at me." "How to Rob" did get Columbia's attention, and everyone else's attention in the music world since it was filled with 50 Cent's plan to "rip off" every hip-hop star around. In his lyrics, 50 Cent warned, "I'll rob Boyz II Men like I'm Michael Bivens/Catch Tyson for half that cash, like Robin Givens." Columbia put 50 Cent's song on the soundtrack to the movie *In Too Deep* (1999), but did little else with their artist.

In May of 2000, 50 Cent's street life caught up with him. While sitting in a friend's car in front of his grandmother's house, another car pulled up, and the driver fired round after round into 50 Cent's body. All told, he was hit nine times, including a bullet to his hip, which shattered the bone, and a bullet to his head. Although 50 Cent survived, the close call was too much for Columbia Records, and the company dropped him from its label. Ever optimistic, the rapper returned to the mixed-tape circuit.

A fan in Slim Shady

In 2002, 50 Cent wrote "Wanksta," the song that would be his ticket to the big time. "Wanksta" was a bouncy party tune, but it was also a direct jab at 50 Cent's archenemy, rapper Ja Rule (1976–). The feud between the two musicians began in 1999, when Ja Rule was robbed and then accused 50 Cent of being involved in the incident. In the song, 50 Cent claims that his rival is merely a gangster wanna-be: "You say you a gangsta, but you never copped nothing'/You say you a wanksta and you need to stop frontin'."

Fifty Cent delivered "Wanksta," along with a few of his other songs, to Paul Rosenberg, manager of the hottest rapper of the moment, Eminem (1972–). Eminem immediately called 50 Cent and asked him to come to Los Angeles. In June of 2002, 50 Cent signed on the dotted line for a reported $1 million, and was the first rapper to be promoted by Shady/Aftermath Records, Eminem's personal record label. According to Serpick, it was a "match made in hip-hop heaven."

Unlike Columbia Records, Shady/Aftermath immediately put 50 Cent to work. Later in 2002, three of 50 Cent's songs, including "Wanksta," appeared on the soundtrack to *8 Mile,* a movie loosely based on the life of Eminem. "Wanksta" received a lot of radio airplay, and listeners lined up to buy a CD by the new rapper. As a result, 50 Cent and Eminem went into the studio to work on 50 Cent's debut disc. Eminem produced several of the songs; other tracks were produced by hip-hop legend Dr. Dre (1965–). The CD, titled *Get Rich or Die Tryin'*, was released in February of 2003, and it immediately broke records. Just days after it debuted, it sold almost one million copies and made it to number-one on the Billboard charts.

Get Rich or Die Tryin'

Get Rich or Die Tryin' sounded like an anthem for 50 Cent's life. He took shots at other rappers in such songs as "U Not Like Me," where his target is Sean "P. Diddy" Combs (1971–), and he included dance cuts, like "In Da Club," which became an immediate hit single. However, as David Browne of *Entertainment Weekly* explained, 50 Cent spent most of *Get Rich or Die Tryin'* "riffing on his crime-ridden past."

Almost all the songs talked about drugs, guns, and death, and all of them were definitely R-rated. Fifty Cent, however, was not apologetic about his lyrics. As he told *Ebony* magazine, "I curse to express how I feel…. The things I've been through made me the way I am

50 Cent performs at the 2003 BET Awards. AP/Wide World Photos. Reproduced by permission.

today." Fifty Cent also addressed his future in *Get Rich or Die Tryin'* and the fact that he is all too eager to reap the rewards of a hip-hop star. In one song, he shares that he has "been patiently waiting for a track to explode." And, according to 50 Cent's "In Da Club," he is "feelin' focus, man, my money on my mind/Got a mil out the deal and I'm still on the grind."

By the end of 2003, *Get Rich or Die Tryin'* had sold more than 6.4 million copies, which made it the best-selling CD of the year. It was also recognized as the biggest number-one debut by a new artist on a major record label. Fifty Cent was nominated for five Grammy Awards (one of the highest achievements in the music industry) and won five World Music Awards. The secret to the CD's success, according to reviewer Ted Kessler, was that behind the clubby dance tunes there was a "cold-blooded seriousness to [50 Cent's] stories … that set him apart." Critics also praised 50 Cent's gritty vocals and commented that his choir-boy smile and his tattooed, well-toned physique probably helped to boost sales, as well.

Member of Da Club

Following the triumph of *Get Rich or Die Tryin'*, 50 Cent became a full-fledged member of the hip-hop club, and started to live the Hollywood lifestyle that goes with it. In October of 2003 the boy from South Jamaica purchased the house of ex-boxing champion Mike Tyson (1966–) for $4.1 million. In addition, since his "bad boy" days were not yet behind him, 50 Cent also purchased a fleet of SUVs, all of which were bulletproof. As he explained to *Ebony*, "No matter how successful you are, you've … gotta take precautions." As added protection, 50 Cent wears a bullet proof vest every day, and insists that his son also wear one. Fifty Cent's fears are not unfounded. In 2002 his longtime friend and mentor Jam Master Jay was shot and killed in his recording studio in Queens, New York.

Fifty Cent does not seem to want to shake his gangster image, but he does intend to channel it into his music and into other projects: "50 Cent is a metaphor for change," 50 Cent explained to Zondra Hughes. In late 2003, 50 Cent and his group G-Unit, short for Guerilla Unit, released their first CD, called *Beg for Mercy*. At the same time, the rapper announced plans to write his autobiography. He was also considering some movie offers. As for the future, 50 Cent was realistic, but hopeful. As he told Serpick, "Trouble seems to find me, so I'm kinda anticipating not everything being beautiful, or going my way. But it feels like it is right now. So far, so good."

For More Information

Periodicals

Browne, David. "Money Talks: It Ain't Nothing But a G Thing for Rapper 50 Cent, Who's Looking to Get Rich or Die Tryin' with the Help of Eminem." *Entertainment Weekly* (February 21, 2003): p. 148.

Brunner, Rob. "Cash of the Titans." *Entertainment Weekly* (May 30, 2003): pp. 26–29.

Drumming, Neil. "4 50 Cent: Rapper's Delight." *Entertainment Weekly* (December 26, 2003): p. 24.

Hughes, Zondra. "The 9 Lives of 50 Cent: Rap Star Survives Shootings, Stabbing and Death Threats." *Ebony* (August 2003): pp. 52–53.

Kessler, Ted. "Shady Business." *New Statesman* (March 31, 2003): p. 43.

Serpick, Evan. "The 50 Cents Piece." *Entertainment Weekly* (February 28, 2003): p. 42–44.

Tyrangiel, Josh. "Rap's Newest Target." *Time* (February 17, 2003): p. 68.

Web Sites

"Eminem Biography." *Shady Soldiers Web site.* http://www.shadysoldiers. com/info/biography.htm (accessed on June 27, 2004).

50 Cent Direct. http://50centdirect.com (accessed on June 27, 2004).

Carly Fiorina

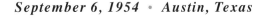

September 6, 1954 • *Austin, Texas*

Chairman and CEO, Hewlett-Packard

AP/Wide World Photos. Reproduced by permission.

u·X·L newsmakers • volume 2

As chairman and chief executive officer (CEO) of Hewlett-Packard (HP), a technology company worth $72 billion, Carly Fiorina is the most powerful woman in American business. Many give credit to the savvy businesswoman for leading the technology titan into the twenty-first century. In 2002 Fiorina cemented her reputation as a risk taker when she engineered a controversial merger between HP and Compaq Computers. After expanding her empire, Fiorina was sitting at the helm of the second largest computer company in the world. By the mid-2000s, however, given HP's shaky numbers, critics wondered if Fiorina's reign would continue. Regardless, her role in history as a trailblazer would remain. When she joined Hewlett-Packard in 1999, Fiorina became the only woman to head a large, publicly held company in the United States.

Steers toward business

Businesswoman Carly Fiorina was born Cara Carleton Sneed on September 6, 1954, in Austin, Texas. Her unique name was the result of family tradition. All the male members of the Sneed family who were named Carleton died while serving in the Civil War (1861–1865). To honor them, one child in each subsequent generation was named either Carleton (if a boy) or Cara Carleton (if a girl). Fiorina's father, Joseph Sneed, was a lawyer and at one time served as deputy attorney general under President Richard M. Nixon (1913–1994). He also served for more than thirty years as an appeals court judge in San Francisco, California. Fiorina's mother, Madelon, was an abstract

> **"Progress is not made by the cynics and doubters. It is made by those who believe everything is possible."**

painter. In 2003, during a ceremony honoring her father's longstanding career, Fiorina credited her parents for inspiring her to excel. "In times of hardship and uncertainty," she observed, as quoted on the *OCE Public Information Office* Web site, "people need a strong internal compass to find their way." Fiorina specifically thanked her father for "always being my true north."

Although Fiorina was raised primarily in the San Francisco Bay area, her father's job caused the family to move quite a bit. She attended at least five high schools all over the world, including Ghana (in Africa) and London, England. Fiorina eventually returned to California to attend Stanford University, located in Palo Alto. Strangely enough, Hewlett-Packard's corporate headquarters are located in Palo Alto, and the future CEO worked in HP's shipping department during a summer break from college. After graduating with a degree in medieval history and philosophy, Fiorina decided to follow in her father's footsteps. She entered law school at the University of California at Los Angeles in 1976. After one semester, however, she dropped out, deciding that a career in law was not for her.

Do You Want to Be Carly Fiorina?

Carly Fiorina has graced the top of *Fortune* magazine's annual list of the most powerful women in business since the ranking was launched in 1998. But in October of 2003, when the magazine polled the other honorees and asked them whether they would like to be in Fiorina's shoes, the answer was consistently "no." Many seemed uncomfortable with the word *power.* As Ann Fudge, CEO of Young & Rubicam (and number 46 on the list), told *Fortune,* "We need to redefine power!" And according to Jenny Ming, president of Old Navy, "Power is in your face and aggressive. I'm not like that."

Definitions aside, according to *Fortune,* by the mid-2000s the trend was that women were regularly being offered positions of power but were not accepting them. And more and more women were leaving their top-level positions or taking short- or long-term breaks. One reason cited was that women were not willing to sacrifice their personal lives, especially time with their children, in order to work a staggering number of hours at their companies. As Jamie Gorelick, former vice chairman of Fannie Mae, commented to *Fortune*, the "secret is that women demand a lot more satisfaction in their lives than men do."

Of course it makes it a lot easier to devote time to a career if one spouse stays at home. Interestingly enough, according to *Fortune,* more than one-third of the women who appeared on the list in 2003 had husbands who were stay-at-home dads. In fact, Carly Fiorina's husband Frank, a former AT&T executive, took an early retirement in 1998 to help focus his energies on his wife's career.

Not only were women turning down or leaving upper level positions in the business world, but business schools were having a difficult time attracting female students. According to a 2002 study by Simmons College of over four thousand teenagers, only 9 percent of girls interviewed expressed an interest in going into business. In addition, women made up only 36 percent of students heading toward a master's degree in business administration (MBA). As Judy Rodin, president of the University of Pennsylvania, explained, young women on her campus regularly commented that "You [career-focused] women work too hard. You're too strung out." Considering that Carly Fiorina starts her day every morning at 4:00, maybe they are right.

Fortune did offer some hope. Young men appeared to be changing their attitudes toward the business world. They, like women, seemed to want a balance between their personal lives and their careers. According to Brenda Barnes, who teaches at the Kellogg School of Management in Chicago, her students have told her that they saw their parents "dedicating themselves to their companies" and that they are not willing to "give their lives over to their jobs." Women executives see this as good news. They predict that if business attitudes change, equality between men and women in the top business spots may become a reality. That reality may be some time coming, however, considering that in 2003 only 8 percent of the top level jobs in corporate America were held by women.

Not sure what to do, Fiorina tried her hand at a number of jobs. She even taught English in Bologna, Italy. It was while working as a receptionist at a New York brokerage firm that her interest in business was sparked. Fiorina decided to go back to school to get a master's degree in business administration (MBA), and in 1980 she graduated from the University of Maryland. Fresh out of graduate school, Fiorina landed a job at the telecommunications giant AT&T as a sales representative. She was quickly promoted to the position of commercial account executive, and was responsible for selling long distance telephone service to federal agencies in the U.S. government.

Lights up Lucent, then snagged by HP

Fiorina's aggressive sales record did not go unnoticed by her employers, who decided that she was definitely management material. As a result, in 1988 she was sent to the prestigious Sloan School of Management at the Massachusetts Institute of Technology to earn a master of science degree in business. While at Sloan, Fiorina met the head of AT&T's Network Systems Group, a manufacturing division of the company that was viewed as sluggish and outdated. Against the advice of colleagues, she decided to transfer to Network Systems, even though it was a low profile area and the move seemed almost certain to stall her career. However, quite the opposite happened. In 1995 Fiorina was appointed as the first woman officer at Network Systems when she was put in charge of North American sales. She became instrumental in carving out new markets for AT&T in the Far East, well before it became commonplace for U.S. businesses to expand on a global scale.

In 1995 AT&T decided to spin off into three separate companies and Fiorina was at the center of the whirlwind. One company would focus on long distance, while NCR Corporation would be the computer company and Lucent Technologies would concentrate on telecommunications and networking equipment, essential for running the Internet. Network Systems was folded into Lucent, and Fiorina was put in charge of revamping the new company. She coordinated Lucent's $3 billion initial public offering (IPO), which is the offering of stock on the open market to the public for the first time. She was also responsible for creating Lucent's flashy marketing image, including its red swirl logo. Lucent quickly became a leader in the networking industry, and Fiorina was given most of the credit. In 1998 she became president of Lucent's Global Service Provider Business, and by year's end Lucent had chalked up $19 billion in revenue. That same year Fiorina was placed at the top of *Fortune* magazine's list of the most powerful women in business.

Other corporations soon took notice of the knowledgeable young professional, including Hewlett-Packard, the grandfather of all computer companies. In July of 1999, HP announced that it had hired Fiorina to be its president and chief executive officer (CEO). The move was remarkable for several reasons. One, HP was a family-owned business, and for the first time it was hiring a president from outside its own ranks. Second, the corporation became the first large U.S. company to place a woman in charge. Third, Fiorina was breaking into Silicon Valley, a region south of San Francisco where there is a concentration of high-tech industries, and until Fiorina came along, the industry had been strictly male-dominated. Although Fiorina was sad to leave AT&T after almost twenty years, she explained to *Electronic News*, "This is a once-in-a-lifetime opportunity for me. Hewlett-Packard is a company of great accomplishment and even greater potential.... I will strive to strike the right balance between reinforcing HP's values and working to reinvent its business."

A house divided

Since its formation in 1939 by Bill Hewlett (1913–2001) and Dave Packard (1912–1996), Hewlett-Packard had grown into one of the preeminent leaders in the computer industry, noted primarily for cornering the printer market. But by the late 1990s it was starting to lose ground, especially to personal computer (PC) giant IBM. The company looked to Fiorina to help it reenergize. As Sam Ginn, a member of HP's board of directors told *Electronic News*, "The board unanimously agreed that she is quite simply the ideal candidate to leverage HP's core strengths in the rapidly changing information-systems industry and to lead this great company well into the new millennium."

Fiorina lost no time cleaning house. She streamlined operations by combining several different divisions into fewer, more manageable units. She also shook up the HP sales staff, telling them to shape up or leave the company. This was a harsh mandate, but at the same time Fiorina was also known for her exceptional leadership skills and for maintaining a loyal employee following. By 2001, however, analysts were wondering if HP's ambitious new CEO had been too aggressive. True, Fiorina had struck some very lucrative deals with Ford Motor Company and Delta Airlines to purchase exclusively from HP, but the corporation's PC sales were still lagging and there had been no major inroads into the world of e-business, as promised. HP remained optimistic. As board member George Keyworth explained to *USA Today,* "In the early summer of 1999, when we were interviewing Carly, we discussed it would take a minimum of three years to turn things around and there would be lots of ups and downs. We are absolutely behind her."

Carly Fioina (left) shakes hands with the chief executive of Compaq, Michael Capellas. Hewlett-Packard purchased Compaq in 2002. AP/Wide World Photo. Reproduced by permission.

The board was divided, however, when Fiorina made a daring announcement in September of 2001. In a further effort to overtake IBM, she proposed to buy Compaq Computers, another faltering leader in the PC industry. The proposed merger could cost up to $25 billion, but Fiorina claimed that the combined assets of the two companies would create an information technology dynamo. Members of both the Hewlett and Packard families balked at the idea, and initially refused to go along with the deal. They eventually relented, and on May 3, 2002, Fiorina successfully engineered the $19 billion consolidation.

Carly claims victory with Compaq

A year-and-a-half after the merger, Fiorina was claiming victory. She told *Fortune* magazine that "the strategy has been vindicated." She also announced that HP "leads in every product category, every geography, and every customer segment in which we participate." The company did look different, and it launched a new ad campaign with the tag line "Everything is possible." It was also branching into new consumer electronics markets, like Tablet PCs and MP3 players, hoping to give new industry leader Dell Computers a run for their money.

But according to business analysts the numbers told a different story. In October of 2003, writer Stephanie Smith observed on the CNN Web site that the "new HP looks a lot like the old HP," and revealed that 80 percent of the company's $4.4 billion profit still came from printer sales. In addition, the morale of HP seemed to be suffering. By January of 2004 seven of HP's top managers had left the company. Some retired, some migrated to the competition, and at least one quit suddenly and without notice. Fiorina remained unfazed, telling *Fortune* that "only 1.7 percent of executives at the vice president level and above have left HP since the merger. That's a pretty small percentage."

Numbers aside, there is no doubt that Fiorina has ranked as a visionary. While at AT&T she helped usher in the era of global business; at Hewlett-Packard she has been at the forefront of new technological ventures. Fiorina has also helped HP become a leader in giving. She launched HP's Technology for Teaching program, which each year awards $10 million in technology grants to U.S. schools from kindergarten through college level. She has also established programs in other countries, including India, to "help bridge the digital divide between technology empowered and technology-excluded communities," as quoted in *PR Newswire*. As a result, in November of 2003 Hewlett-Packard was honored by the international nonprofit humanitarian organization Concern Worldwide for "its commitment to spearheading educational initiatives around the world."

For More Information

Books

"Carly Fiorina Biography." *Business Leader Profiles for Students.* Vol. 2. Farmington Hills, MI: Gale Group, 2002.

Periodicals

"Concern Worldwide US Presents 'Seeds of Hope' Award to HP's Carly Fiorina." *PR Newswire* (November 5, 2003).

"Fiorina Named HP President and CEO." *Electronic News* (July 26, 1999): p. 14.

Lashinsky, Adam. "Power 25: No. 19 Carly Fiorina, Hewlett Packard." *Fortune* (August 11, 2003): p. 78.

Lashinsky, Adam. "Wall Street to Carly: Prove It! HP Talks Up a Turnaround, but Investors Don't Buy It—Yet." *Fortune* (January 12, 2004): p. 36.

Scardino, Marjorie. "Carly Fiorina: Inventing a New Hewlett-Packard." *Time* (April 26, 2004): p. 72.

Swartz, Jon. "Another Thumbs Down for H-P Deal." *USA Today* (November 8, 2001).

Web sites

"Carly Most Powerful Woman—Again." *CNNMoney.com* (September 29, 2003). http://money.cnn.com/2003/09/29/technology/fortune_women/index.htm (accessed on May 21, 2004).

"Court of Appeals Honors Judge Joseph T. Sneed." *OCE Public Information Office* (December 9, 2003). http://www.ce9.uscourts.gov/web/OCELibra.nsf/0/bc0e84a3abe7cc0688256df9000124fa?OpenDocument (accessed on May 21, 2004).

La Monica, Paul R. "Fiorina Strikes Back." *CNNMoney.com* (November 21, 2002). http://money.cnn.com/2002/11/18/technology/comdex_fiorina (accessed on May 21, 2004).

Smith, Stephanie. "Can HP Find Its Way?" *CNNMoney.com* (October 2003). http://money.cnn.com/best/magazine_archive/2003/10/SEL-02.html (accessed on May 21, 2004).

Cornelia Funke

© 2004 Landov LLC. All rights reserved. Reproduced by permission.

1958 • Dorsten, Westphalia, Germany

Author, illustrator

For years Cornelia Funke has been one of the best-known and best-selling children's authors in Germany. In fact, many people have called her the German J. K. Rowling. Americans, however, were not exposed to Funke's work until 2002, when her book *Herr der Diebe* was translated into English and released by Scholastic Press as *The Thief Lord*. The response was immediate and overwhelming. Like their German counterparts, young American readers gobbled up the fantastic tale of two orphans set loose among the canals and streets of Venice, Italy. The book made every major bestseller list and won countless awards. It also established Funke as a storyteller on an international scale, since the book has since been published in nearly forty countries. In October of 2003 Funke released her second book in the United States, *Inkheart*. *Publisher's Weekly* called it "delectably transfixing," and readers were left clamoring for more of their favorite new author.

Illustrator becomes author

Cornelia Funke was born in 1958 in Dorsten, Westphalia, located in the central region of Germany. Funke, who spoke with Sue Corbett of the *Miami Herald,* explained that her last name is pronounced FOON-kah. She also mentioned that in the United States "people say 'Funky,' and I rather like that." Funke did not set out to be a writer. When she was eighteen years old she left Dorsten to study at the University of Hamburg, where she earned a degree in education theory. Not sure what to do after graduation, Funke decided to take a course in book illustration at the Hamburg State College of Design.

> "If I was a book, I would like to be a library book, so I would be taken home by all different sorts of kids. A library book, I imagine, is a happy book."

Funke started out designing board games and illustrating books for other authors. After illustrating for several years, however, she began to lose interest in her job. "I was, I have to admit, bored by the stories I had to illustrate," Funke explained in a *Bookwrap* video interview online. Instead, she wanted to draw pictures for books that were exciting, books about dragons and adventure. She recalled that one night, at the age of twenty-eight, she started to write her own story. The illustrator-turned-author did not suffer the usual trials of first-time writers. She sent her manuscript out to four German publishing houses and all four wanted to publish it.

Funke's earliest books, most of which she illustrated herself, were short and aimed at younger readers of about eight years old. Her first longer, chapter book for older children was *Drachenreiter* (*Dragonrider*), published in Germany in 1997. It was followed in 2000 by *Herr der Diebe* (*The Thief Lord*). The book was a phenomenal success in Germany, but Funke was not satisfied. She was determined to take a shot at the English-language market, where she knew her stories would have a chance to be read by a wider audience. Funke turned to her cousin, Oliver Latsch, and asked him to translate *Herr*

Cornelia Funke's Favorite Books

In many of her interviews, writer Cornelia Funke describes herself as a passionate reader. And, as she revealed in an *AudioFile* interview, one of her goals as an author is to "try to awaken the passion for reading in children and adults." In *Inkheart,* one way Funke accomplishes this goal is by introducing her audience to classic works of fiction. Each chapter begins with a quote from a book, and there are references to books such as *The Wind in the Willows* by Scottish author Kenneth Grahame (1859–1932) sprinkled throughout the text. In an article posted on the *Guardian Unlimited* Web site, Funke revealed her own "favourite bedtime stories," many of which are mentioned in *Inkheart.*

1. *Tom Sawyer* by Mark Twain.
2. *The BFG* by Roald Dahl.
3. *What Witch* by Eva Ibbotson.
4. *Just So Stories* by Rudyard Kipling.
5. *Jim Button and Luke the Engine Driver* by Michael Ende.
6. *Peter Pan* by J. M. Barrie.
7. *The Brothers Lionheart* by Astrid Lindgren.
8. *The War of the Buttons* by Louis Peraud.
9. *The Wizard of Oz* by L. Frank Baum.
10. *The Princess Bride* by William Goldman.

der Diebe into English. With manuscript in hand, she made the rounds of the top English publishers.

Thief Lord steals the hearts of millions

Several companies showed an interest, but at the same time the fates were actively at work at The Chicken House, a new book publisher in England. The Chicken House was founded in 2000 by Barry Cunningham, who had a long career in publishing and was known for taking chances on new writers. In fact, it was Cunningham who first decided to publish the Harry Potter series after British author J. K. Rowling (c. 1966–) was turned down by countless other publishers. In this case, Funke did not go to Cunningham. Cunningham went looking for her, after he received a letter from an eleven-year-old girl in England named Clara, asking why her favorite author (Cornelia Funke) was not published in English. Clara was bilingual, she spoke both German and English, so she had been enjoying Funke's books for several years.

Cunningham tracked down Funke's agent, read the manuscript, and immediately bought the English-language rights for *Herr der Diebe* and for *Drachenreiter.* In July of 2000 *The Thief Lord* was published in England. It sold out in just ten days, an unheard-of phenomenon for a children's book. Two years later Funke's story debuted in the United States. Critics heaped praise on *The Thief Lord,* calling it an immediate classic. Readers agreed, and the book reached the *New York Times* bestseller list, where it remained comfortably perched for twenty-five weeks. *The Thief Lord* was named a best book of the year by many publications, including *School Library Journal* and *Parenting Magazine.* It also won a slew of awards, including the prestigious Mildred L. Batchelder Award, which is presented annually by the American Library Association to the best book originally published in a foreign language and then translated and published in the United States.

Part *Peter Pan* and part *Robin Hood* and *Oliver Twist, The Thief Lord* is set against the backdrop of Venice, Italy. Rebecca Sinkler of the *New York Times* called the book a "love song to the city and its splendors." In fact, Venice is one of Funke's favorite destinations, and she was inspired to write the story during one of her many visits. "I wanted to tell children that there is a place in this world that is real and full of history, but also contains magic and mystery," she explained to Trudy Wyss in an interview on the Borders Books Web site. The many alleyways and canals of Venice were perfect for the story because, as Funke told Wyss, "there are hundreds of hiding places."

At the story's center are two orphans, twelve-year-old Prosper and his five-year-old brother, Bo, who run away from Hamburg to Venice because their aunt and uncle want to separate them. When they arrive in the strange city, they are taken in by a band of young pickpockets and thieves who are led by Scipio, the thirteen-year-old masked Thief Lord. The boys live comfortably enough with their new-found friends in an abandoned movie theater until they discover they are being tracked by an investigator hired by their aunt and uncle. They also run into trouble when the gang is hired to steal a wooden horse's wing that long ago was broken off a magical carousel. The carousel has the power to make "adults out of children and children out of adults."

Written from the heart

Readers were spellbound by the many twists and turns in the plot of *The Thief Lord,* and Funke left her audience wanting more. They were rewarded in October of 2003 when Scholastic Press, her American

Cornelia Funke poses with her book, **Inkheart.** © 2004 Landov LLC. All rights reserved. Reproduced by permission.

publisher, released *Inkheart.* There is a gleam in Funke's eye when she talks about this book, which she believes to be one of her best efforts. As she explained in the *Bookwrap* video, she put the "blood of her heart" into writing it: "There are those people who love books and are greedy for books and the rustling of paper and the printed letter and I wanted to write about this. This lust for the printed word. And I think *Inkheart* is all about that. The enchantment that comes from books."

Good authors make books come alive for their readers. In *Inkheart,* twelve-year-old Meggie loves books so much that she regularly falls asleep with them. Her father, Mo, teases her, saying, "I'm sure it must be very comfortable sleeping with a hard, rectangular thing like that under your head." But Meggie enjoys taking her books to bed because the books whisper their stories to her at night. Books are also important to her father, who earns his living by traveling across the country repairing and caring for old volumes. He does not, however, read to his daughter because of a secret power he possesses: if Mo reads a book aloud, its characters leave the pages and enter the real world. Mo discovered his gift several years earlier, when he released characters from the book *Inkheart.* One of them, named Capricorn, is so evil that his heart is said to be made of ink. Capricorn hunts down Mo because he wants to destroy *Inkheart,* ensuring that he will never return to its pages.

The success of *Inkheart* followed that of *The Thief Lord.* The book debuted at number nine on the *New York Times* bestseller list and stayed on the list into 2004. It also received rave reviews. *Publisher's*

Weekly enthused that "readers will be captivated by the chilling and thrilling world [Funke] has created." James Neal Webb of *BookPage* went so far as to call it "a magical, life-altering volume."

Funke on film

To promote her books, in November of 2003 Funke left Hamburg and her children, Anna and Ben, and went on a U.S. book tour. (The character of Bo in *The Thief Lord* was based on Ben.) She was interviewed on television and radio and visited many bookstores across the United States. In her *Bookwrap* video interview Funke commented about the American children she met on tour, and how open and curious they were. "It was great fun to meet them," she said. "I was especially enchanted by the book maniacs in America. I didn't know there was so many here…. And I have to confess this kind of book passion I have only met in America."

Funke revealed to the *Miami Herald* that there are two sequels planned for *Inkheart*. The second in the series, called *Inkblood,* has already been written and is being translated from the German, with an expected release date of 2005. In addition, there are movies in the works based on *The Thief Lord* and on the *Inkheart* trilogy. Once her books hit the big screen, Funke, already a beloved writer, will no doubt become a writing phenomenon. And there is also no doubt that there are many more books to come from her pen. As she told Wyss, "Writing is my passion…. I couldn't live without it."

For More Information

Books

Funke, Cornelia. *Dragon Rider.* New York: Scholastic Books, 2004.
Funke, Cornelia. *Inkheart.* New York: Scholastic Books, 2003.
Funke, Cornelia. *The Thief Lord.* New York: Scholastic Books, 2002.

Periodicals

Corbett, Sue. "Author on Her Way to Fame; Could Be Next J. K. Rowling." *Miami Herald* (December 2, 2003).
Review of *Inkheart. Publisher's Weekly* (July 21, 2003): p. 196.
Review of *The Thief Lord. Publisher's Weekly* (June 24, 2002): p. 57.
Sinkler, Rebecca Pepper. "Children's Books: Theft in Venice." *New York Times* (November 17, 2003).

Webb, James Neal. "Characters Come to Life in Fast-Paced Fantasy." *BookPage* (November 2003).

Web sites

"Cornelia Funke Biography." *Scholastic Books: Book Central.* http://www.scholastic.com/titles/authors/Cornelia_funke.htm (accessed on May 25, 2004.

"Cornelia Funke's Favourite Bedtime Stories." *Guardian Unlimited (U.K.).* http://books.guardian.co.uk/top10s/top10/0,6109,1063558,00.html (accessed on May 27, 2004).

Inkheart by Cornelia Funke (video clip interview). *Bookstream Inc./Book-wrap.* http://a1110.g.akamai.net/7/1110/5507/v002/bookstream.download.akamai.com/5507/bw/bs/0439531640/b1/default_wm.htm (accessed on May 26, 2004).

"Talking with Cornelia Funke: Cornelia Funke Interview." *AudioFile* http://www.audiofilemagazine.com/features/A1222.html (accessed on May 27, 2004).

Wyss, Trudy. "Hey American Kids, Meet Cornelia Funke: A Beloved German Children's Author Makes Her U.S. Debut." *Borders Books.* http://www.bordersstores.com/features/feature.jsp?file=funke (accessed on May 27, 2004).

Neil Gaiman

AP/Wide World Photos. Reproduced by permission.

November 10, 1960 • *Portchester, England*

Writer

Neil Gaiman is an extraordinarily imaginative writer who works in a variety of formats, writing graphic novels (or, book-length comics), short stories, novels, children's books, and scripts for television and films. His works are classified in a number of different genres, from horror to fantasy to science fiction, and often he jumps from one genre to another within a single work. Gaiman understands the conventional rules of writing fiction, particularly comic books, but he rarely follows such rules, choosing instead to pursue the winding paths of his imagination. Gaiman has achieved rock-star status among his millions of fans, and is best known for his *Sandman* series of comic books. He began writing *Sandman* installments in the late 1980s, developing a passionate following along the way. After a break of several years from *Sandman,* he published the graphic novel *Sandman: Endless Nights* in 2003. In October of that year, *Endless Nights* reached number twenty on the *New York Times* bestseller list, a rare feat for a comic book. Gaiman has also achieved success with a novella, or short novel, for young adults, titled *Coraline*. The novel earned a number of prestigious awards, including the Hugo and Nebula awards for outstanding works of science fiction and fantasy, and the Bram Stoker award, which is given to exceptional works of horror.

A reader becomes a writer

Gaiman was born in Portchester, England, in 1960. His mother, a pharmacist, and his father, the director of a company, encouraged their young son's reading habits, although even without such encouragement Gaiman would probably have been an avid reader. He devoured every book he could get his hands on as a child, working his way through the

> **"**All my life, I've felt that I was getting away with something because I was just making things up and writing them down, and that one day there would be a knock, and a man with a clipboard would be standing there and say, 'It says here you've just been making things up all these years. Now it's time to go off and work in a bank.'**"**

entire local children's library and partway through the adult collection as well. In an interview on the *KAOS2000 Magazine* Web site, Gaiman explained that he carried a book with him wherever he went: "Before weddings, bar mitzvahs, funerals and anything else where you're actually meant to not be reading, my family would frisk me and take the book away." He read books in a number of different genres, especially comics, and he was particularly drawn to science fiction and fantasy works. While preparing for his own bar mitzvah, a Jewish ceremony marking a young man's transition to the world of adulthood, Gaiman became entranced by religious and mystical Jewish writings.

As a teenager Gaiman began to outgrow the comic books he had loved as a child. Faced with a lack of comic books aimed at a more mature audience, Gaiman decided to fill that need himself. He wanted to write comic books when he grew up, although at the time he had no idea how to accomplish that goal. After graduating from high school in 1977, Gaiman became a journalist. He wrote articles for a number of British newspapers and magazines, including the *Sunday Times,* the *Observer,* and *Time Out.* In 1983 he and partner Mary McGrath had their first child, named Michael. In March of 1985 Gaiman wed McGrath, and that same year their daughter, Holly, was born. During that time Gaiman began writing short stories, including such titles as "How to Be a Barbarian," "How to Spot a Psycho," and "Jokers through History."

In the early 1980s Gaiman began reading the works of esteemed British comic book writer Alan Moore, author of such landmark works as *Swamp Thing* and *Watchmen.* He told *Authors and Artist for Young Adults (AAYA)*: "Moore's work convinced me that you really could do work in comics that had the same amount of intelligence, the same amount of passion, the same amount of quality that you could put in any other medium," such as novels, short stories, or films. While comic books had been around since the 1930s, the development of the graphic novel as a serious form of literature was relatively recent, and the rules for the genre were still being written. Gaiman was drawn to the experimental nature of adult-oriented comic books and graphic novels, and in the mid-1980s he began writing comics. He wrote several issues of a series called *2000AD* before publishing the graphic novel *Violent Cases* in 1987. *Violent Cases* depicts a grown man's childhood recollections, with a visit to an elderly doctor as the starting point of those memories. While treating the four-year-old child for a broken arm, the doctor shares vivid stories from decades earlier, when the infamous gangster Al Capone was his patient.

After publishing *Violent Cases,* which was illustrated by his frequent collaborator Dave McKean, Gaiman came to the attention of celebrated publisher DC Comics, home of Batman and Superman. His next work, a three-part series called *Black Orchid,* was published by DC Comics, the first of Gaiman's many works to find a home there. The series revisits a character from DC's history, the crime-fighting heroine named in the title. Black Orchid is quite different from the

Not Comic Books: The Stories and Novels of Neil Gaiman

While Neil Gaiman initially and enduringly captured the imaginations of millions of readers with his *Sandman* comics and other graphic novels, he has also applied his seemingly endless energy to works of prose, namely novels and short stories.

Gaiman began writing short stories before ever penning a comic book, and some of his stories and story-poems have been collected into the volumes *Angels and Visitations* (1993) and *Smoke and Mirrors* (1998). As with his other writings, these collections range across many genres, from fantasy, science fiction, and horror, to comedy and mystery.

Gaiman's first novel was a comedic collaboration with English writer Terry Pratchett. *Good Omens: The Nice and Accurate Prophecies of Agnes Nutter, Witch* (1990) was written over a period of several weeks in 1989, with Gaiman and Pratchett sharing their contributions over the phone, each working hard to make the other laugh hysterically. The novel uses slapstick comedy to address the most serious of subjects: the end of humankind. In 2003 *Good Omens* was named one of England's one hundred "best-loved novels" in a poll conducted by the British Broadcasting Corporation (BBC).

In 1996 Gaiman published *Neverwhere,* a novel that came about after he had written the script for a six-part BBC series with the same title. Dissatisfied with the many compromises made during the filming of the series, Gaiman opted to regain control of his ideas by issuing the work as a novel. In an interview on the *Writers Write* Web site, Gaiman related that every time a major alteration was made to his script during the production of the series, he would think to himself, "It's OK, I'll put it back in the novel." The book explores the adventures of Londoner Richard Mayhew, who encounters a girl named Door, a visitor from an other-

typical female characters in comic books; Gaiman described her to *AAYA* as "vaguely feminist, ecological, essentially nonviolent. I liked the fact that at the end she doesn't get mad and start hitting people." For his next venture, DC asked Gaiman to revive another old character, and Gaiman chose the little-known Sandman, a character that originated in the 1940s. DC hired Gaiman to write a monthly serial featuring the Sandman, a career move intended to build the writer's reputation. Much to the surprise of both Gaiman and DC Comics, the *Sandman* series was an immediate hit.

The Lord of Dreams

Gaiman's first *Sandman* installment came out in 1989, and over the next eight years a total of seventy-five issues were released. With each new comic, Gaiman elaborated on the complex universe surrounding the Sandman, complete with myths explaining the origin of that uni-

worldly place called London Below. Door has the ability to travel between the two worlds, the real London and the fantastical underground London, and Mayhew accompanies her, helping her flee a pair of brutal assassins. Attempting once again to bring his vision of *Neverwhere* to the screen, Gaiman sold the rights to his novel to Jim Henson Productions, the company best known as the home of the Muppets.

For *Stardust,* Gaiman collaborated with artist Charles Vess to produce a short, richly illustrated fantasy novel. Described by many as an adult fairy story, *Stardust* tells the romantic tale of a young man battling powerful foes to retrieve a fallen star promised to his beloved. *Stardust* was initially released as a four-part illustrated series by DC Comics in 1997 and 1998; one year later, Spike Books issued a one-volume version without illustrations. Critics raved, fans went wild, and plans were soon underway to make a *Stardust* movie.

In 2001 Gaiman released *American Gods,* perhaps his best-known work outside of his graphic novels. A typical Gaiman hodge-podge of fantasy, science fiction, horror, and mythology, *American Gods* tells the story of ancient European gods who accompanied waves of immigrants to the shores of the United States, only to be discarded and ignored in modern society. They have been replaced by American-bred gods such as Media and Technology, and the old-time gods are fed up and looking for a fight with their newer counterparts. *American Gods* connected with Gaiman's many fans and earned new fans as well, all of whom propelled the book to a spot on the *New York Times* bestseller list. The novel won numerous awards, including the Hugo, Nebula, Locus, SFX (for outstanding works of science fiction and fantasy), and the Bram Stoker award for distinguished works of horror. While Gaiman established his reputation with his groundbreaking work in comics, he has cemented his legacy by applying his creativity to every existing genre and by inventing a few new ones as well.

verse. Myths are stories handed down through the ages, often used to explain a culture's practices or beliefs. In the world of the *Sandman,* a family of seven immortal, godlike creatures, known as the Endless, engage in cosmic struggles. Each of the Endless represents a different element of human emotions and experience—Dream, Desire, Despair, Destiny, Delirium (formerly Delight), Destruction, and Death. Known by a variety of names, including Sandman, Morpheus, Lord of the Dreaming, and Master of Story, Dream wanders through places both earthbound and otherworldly. Tall, thin, and pale, with spiky black hair, Dream is the ruler of the Dreaming, a sort of parallel universe that exists alongside earthly reality. Humans can enter the Dreaming only while sleeping. Dream is a mysterious figure, unknowable even to the most devoted readers. *AAYA* quoted Gaiman as saying, "He's definitely not human. I mean, he is the personification of dreams. He's the king of the dreaming place where you close your eyes each night and go. And whether he's [good or evil] depends an awful lot on where you're standing. From his own standards, he is always acting for the best, but his moral code and his point of view are not human."

Gaiman approached the *Sandman* stories in an everything-but-the-kitchen-sink frame of mind, incorporating mythologies of his own invention as well as ancient Greek myths. He also found inspiration in the mystical Jewish writings he had studied as a youth. He didn't stop there, however, as he explained to Scott Brown in *Entertainment Weekly:* "I just kept adding things, seeing if it would hold. I thought, Let's put Shakespeare in there. Okay, that worked. Well, surely I won't be able to add the Norse gods.... No, that worked too. But I certainly won't get away with angels." As Brown pointed out, "He got away with angels, and more." The *Sandman* stories are complicated, sophisticated works written on a grand scale. Gaiman's rich, multi-layered universe presents a challenge to readers; these are not simple stories that can be grasped immediately. Gaiman's *Sandman* comics broke new ground in many ways. They brought female fans to the world of comics, a genre typically read mostly by men, and in addition they converted legions of readers who had never before considered comics to be serious literature. Gaiman's comics have won numerous awards, many of which are usually reserved for traditional prose works—short stories, novels, and the like—rather than comic books. In *Entertainment Weekly,* Brown quoted comics writer Moore, the object of Gaiman's admiration from early on, who said of Gaiman's *Sandman* creation: "It's a perfect legend. It's so good that it shouldn't really even have a writer. It should be one of those stories that's just always been there."

Throughout the initial eight-year run of the *Sandman* serials, DC Comics periodically collected several issues for publication as a graphic novel. The first such collection, *Sandman: Preludes and Nocturnes,* introduces the reader to Sandman's universe. *Sandman: The Wake* includes the final installment of the series that concluded in 1996. Gaiman's many devoted fans felt crushed when the series ended, but the author revisited the character in several later works. In 1999 he released *Sandman: The Dream Hunters,* a collaboration with illustrator Yoshitaka Amano that retells a Japanese story titled "The Fox, the Monk, and the Mikado of All Night's Dreaming." A long-awaited continuation of the series appeared in 2003, with *Sandman: Endless Nights* garnering rave reviews, earning a number of awards, and securing a spot on the *New York Times* bestseller list. *Endless Nights* is a collection of seven separate stories, each devoted to one of the Endless and each illustrated by a different artist. Gaiman told Jeff Zaleski of *Publishers Weekly* that he takes pride in the variety of genres explored in *Endless Nights:* "Do you know what the coolest thing about Endless Nights is?… Not one of those stories is even in the same genre as any of the other stories."

"Warping young minds"

The Sandman also made an appearance in works Gaiman wrote for a young adult audience, showing up in a small role in *Books of Magic,* a collection of four comic books concerning the world of illusion and trickery. Sandman's sister, Death, played a prominent role in the *Sandman* spinoff *Death: The High Cost of Living.* In a once-per-century visit to Earth, Death helps a suicidal teenager discover new reasons for living.

In 2003 Gaiman released another work for young adult readers, the novel *Coraline.* In this work the title character, a young child, discovers a doorway in her new house that leads to a matching home in a different world. In that other world, a set of parents with pale skin and black button eyes ask Coraline to stay with them and be their daughter. Realizing that her own mother and father are in need of rescuing, Coraline then engages in a dangerous struggle with the "other mother" to retrieve her parents. Gaiman has also written books for young children, including the picture book *The Day I Swapped My Dad for Two Goldfish,* published in 1997. In that story, young Nathan trades his father for a bowl of goldfish. His mother, unhappy with the outcome of the trade, forces Nathan to retrieve his father, and the boy must engage in a series of exchanges to get his parent back. During 2003 Gaiman published another children's story, *The Wolves in the Walls,* in which the young heroine Lucy must convince her family that their home is being taken over by wolves. "I love writing children's books," Gaiman told Phil Anderson of *KAOS2000.* "I think I will always write children's books. I love warping young minds."

Gaiman is an extremely prolific writer who has created a long list of works in an impressive variety of genres. In addition to his comic books, graphic novels, and works for young people, he has also written several successful novels, including *Neverwhere,* which began as the script for a six-part series for British television, and *American Gods,* a bestseller in the United States that depicts a struggle between the European gods of ancient origin and the newer, more arrogant American gods. Gaiman has written numerous scripts for television and movies—in some cases working on film adaptations of his own works—with his best-known work being the English-language script for the highly praised Japanese animated film *Princess Mononoke.* During the summer of 2003 Gaiman returned to the comic book genre with the series *1602.* Set in seventeenth-century England, this series is published by Marvel, a major rival of DC Comics.

At any given time Gaiman juggles several projects, and he also makes time for extensive book tours. His public appearances draw record numbers of fans, more than most authors, and he inspires in his followers the kind of adoration generally not experienced by authors. Fans have been known to faint at his book signings, and at least two have asked Gaiman to draw on a portion of their body, so they can then have his writing tattooed onto their skin. When not traveling the world to promote his works, Gaiman spends much of his time writing at his large Victorian home located near Minneapolis, a home he shares with McGrath and their youngest child, Maddy.

For More Information

Books

Authors and Artists for Young Adults, Vol. 42. Detroit: Gale, 2002.

Periodicals

Brown, Scott. "The Best Comic Book Ever Returns." *Entertainment Weekly* (October 3, 2003): p. 36.

Zaleski, Jeff. "Comics! Books! Film! The Arts and Ambitions of Neil Gaiman." *Publishers Weekly* (July 28, 2003): p. 46.

Web Sites

Anderson, Phil. "Interview with: Neil Gaiman." *KAOS2000 Magazine.* http://www.kaos2000.net/interviews/neilgaiman99.html (accessed on July 6, 2004).

Krewson, John. "Neil Gaiman." *The Onion A.V. Club.* http://www.theonion avclub.com/feature/index.php?issue=3504&f=1 (accessed on July 3, 2004).

Neil Gaiman Official Web site. http://www.neilgaiman.com/index.asp (accessed on July 6, 2004).

Richards, Linda. "Neil Gaiman." *January Magazine.* http://www.january magazine.com/profiles/gaiman.html (accessed on July 3, 2004).

White, Claire E. "A Conversation with Neil Gaiman." *Writers Write.* http://www.writerswrite.com/journal/mar99/gaiman.htm (accessed on July 3, 2004).

Sonia Gandhi

AP/Wide World Photos. Reproduced by permission.

December 9, 1947 • *Orbassano, Italy*

Politician

The story should have had a fairy-tale ending: a beautiful young girl meets her handsome Prince Charming, has two children, and lives happily every after. In 1968, however, when Sonia Maino married Rajiv Gandhi of India, the fairy tale was only half realized. She snagged a handsome prince, but she also inherited the troubled history of his country. Rajiv Gandhi was a member of a family that had ruled India since the 1940s. His grandfather, Jawaharlal Nehru, was India's first prime minister, and his mother, Indira Gandhi, held that office throughout the 1970s. Rajiv himself briefly served as prime minister in the 1980s, but was assassinated in 1991 as he attempted to reclaim the post. Almost a decade after her husband's death, Sonia Gandhi reluctantly followed in her famous family's footsteps by entering politics. In 2004, after serving as president of India's Congress Party, she was called upon by members of Parliament to take up the reins of prime minister. Gandhi shocked the nation, and the world, when she declined. Members of the opposition breathed a sigh of relief, but others feared that the Nehru-Gandhi dynasty had come to an end.

Love at first sight

Sonia Gandhi was born Sonia Maino on December 9, 1947, in the small village of Orbassano, just outside Turin, Italy. She was raised in a traditional Roman Catholic household, and her parents, Stefano and Paolo, were working class people. Stefano was a building contractor who owned his own medium-sized construction business; Paolo took care of the family's three daughters. When Sonia was eighteen years old, her

---

"Power in itself has never attracted me, nor has position been my goal."

---

father sent her to Cambridge, England, to study English. He did not know that his oldest daughter's life was about to change forever.

In 1965, just a year after arriving in England, Sonia met a young Indian student named Rajiv Gandhi (1944–1991), who was studying mechanical engineering at Cambridge University. According to Sonia Gandhi, it was love at first sight. The courtship, however, lasted three years, perhaps because Rajiv was from one of the most famous families in India, if not the world. Sonia's parents were reluctant to have her become involved in such a different culture, and Sonia herself was nervous about meeting Rajiv's famous mother, Indira Gandhi (1917–1984), who was considered to be the "first lady" of India. Indira Gandhi's father, Jawaharlal Nehru (1889–1964), became the country's first prime minister after India claimed its independence from Great Britain in 1947, and Gandhi worked closely with him until his death. In 1965 Indira Gandhi was poised to fill Nehru's shoes.

Sonia's fears were quickly overcome as she and Indira became fast friends. In 1968, Sonia and Rajiv were married in a simple ceremony in New Delhi, India; Sonia wore the same pink sari her mother-in-law had worn at her own wedding many years before. A sari is a

India's Parliament Explained

India's government is based on the British parliamentary system. The Parliament, or ruling legislative body, is divided into two houses: the upper house, called the Rajya Sabha, consists of a maximum of 250 members; the lower house, known as the Lok Sabha, is composed of no more than 545 members. As in the United States, members of each house are elected to office, and they represent constituents who reside in a particular state. There are fourteen states in India. Legislative elections are held every five years. Following the election, if one party receives a majority of votes, one member is voted in by the party as prime minister. If one party does not achieve a majority of votes, members negotiate with other parties in order to form what is known as a coalition government.

traditional dress that consists of several yards of cloth draped around the waist and shoulders. Following the wedding Sonia and Rajiv moved in with Indira Gandhi, who by this time had become prime minister. Sonia's relationship with Indira deepened, and ultimately she became the faithful and obedient daughter-in-law, in charge of running the household. This meant that although Gandhi came into the marriage a modern woman of the West, she soon traded her miniskirts for saris and steeped herself in Indian culture. She even learned to speak Hindi, the official language of India.

Rajiv reluctantly enters politics

While Sonia Gandhi served as hostess at state functions and received visiting dignitaries along with her mother-in-law, Rajiv Gandhi remained relatively removed from politics. After leaving Cambridge, he did not go into engineering; instead he pursued his passion for flying and became a commercial airline pilot for Indian Airlines. The heir to the political throne was expected to be Rajiv's younger brother, Sanjay (1946–1980). As a result, the Gandhis lived in relative peace and quiet, while raising their two children, Rahul and Priyanka, away from the glare of the media.

In the meantime, the 1970s became the Indira Gandhi decade in India. The Indian public revered her, calling her *Mataji,* meaning revered mother. Her political opponents, however, viewed her as a sometimes ruthless leader who seemed determined to form a dictatorship. She even caused dissension within her own political party, the Congress Party (CP). The CP was particularly popular in India, because its early members were major figures in the fight for independence from Great Britain. As a result, the party controlled India's government for most of the twentieth century. In 1969, however, Gandhi split the CP; her splinter group was eventually called the Congress-I Party, the "I" standing for Indira.

By the late 1970s Sanjay had become Gandhi's primary policy adviser, and in 1980 he officially entered politics by winning a seat in Parliament. Before Sanjay had a chance to fulfill his destiny, however, he was killed in a flying accident. A stunned Indira Gandhi begged her older son to join the family's political ranks. Sonia Gandhi was vehemently opposed to the idea, fearing that her husband might be injured or killed, given the explosive nature of Indian politics. After several long discussions, however, the couple jointly agreed that Rajiv should quit his job with the airlines. Although Sonia Gandhi was not pleased, she was a dutiful wife and supported her husband's decision. In 1981 Rajiv ran successfully for Parliament and took over the seat vacated by his brother. He served as the representative from the Amethi district of Uttar Pradesh, a state in northern India populated by approximately 160 million inhabitants.

A grieving widow

In 1984 the Gandhi family, and India, was shaken to its very core when Indira Gandhi was assassinated by two of her own bodyguards. Tensions had been escalating for some time between various Indian religious sects, including Muslims, Hindus, and Sikhs. Earlier in the year, Sikh militants had stockpiled weapons in their sacred Golden Temple, assuming that the government would not dare to enter their holy sanctuary. Gandhi, however, sent troops to storm the temple, which resulted in the deaths of many militants. In retaliation, Gandhi's bodyguards, who were Sikhs, shot and killed the prime minister in her own home. Just hours after the shootings, Rajiv Gandhi was sworn in as his mother's replacement.

Sonia Gandhi, resigned to the fact that her husband must lead his country, became his vigilant supporter and submerged herself in the role of a prime minister's wife. She became an art historian and

Manmohan Singh: India's Newest Prime Minister

India's newest prime minister, Dr. Manmohan Singh, was born into a family of very modest means on September 26, 1932, in Gah, West Punjab (now Pakistan). After earning degrees in economics from Cambridge University in England and from Punjab University, he spent the next thirty years working as a quiet but very key player in Indian politics. In the 1980s Singh served as the head of the Reserve Bank of India, and in 1991 he became the country's finance minister in the Congress Party-led government of Narasimha Rao (1921–), which was in power until 1996.

When he took the post, India was in disastrous financial straits, but during his tenure Singh became the mastermind behind the country's economic reform movement. He opened up the country to outside investors for the first time, and ended regulations that had kept India tied to the past. For example, Singh dissolved the "license Raj," which required private businesses to seek government approval before making almost any decision. By the end of the 1990s, with Singh's help, India was well on its way to economic recovery.

Perhaps more remarkable, however, was that throughout the decades of scandal that rocked the Indian government, Singh retained an incredibly "squeaky clean" reputation. In fact, in 2002 he was awarded the Outstanding Parliamentarian Award. And in May of 2004, when it was announced that he would be taking on the post of prime minister, Singh was given support across the board from representatives of the various Indian parties.

Singh has been married since 1958 and has three daughters. In addition to playing an active role in government, he is also a respected professor of economics and a published author. He is a member of the Sikh faith; when he became prime minister, he became the first Sikh to hold the country's top government position.

worked with a team at the National Gallery in New Delhi to restore Indian landscapes. She also collected and edited letters that had been sent between Indira Gandhi and her father, Jawaharlal Nehru, which were ultimately published in the late 1980s and early 1990s. Despite Sonia Gandhi's successes, however, her husband Rajiv was a less-than-successful ruler. He was never able to match the popularity of his famous mother, and his administration was plagued by one problem after another, including charges of illegal arms dealings. As a result, in 1989 Rajiv Gandhi was voted out of office.

In the 1991 elections, Rajiv hit the campaign trail determined to reclaim his family's title. In an uncharacteristic move, security was light. Following his mother's death, Rajiv had taken to wearing a bulletproof vest and had surrounded himself with bodyguards. On this trip, however, his goal was to reconnect with the masses. Unfortunately, the lack of security would prove to be his undoing. On May 22,

1991, while swinging through Tamil Nadu, a key state in south India, he was killed by a young female assassin. The woman was a member of the Tamil Tigers, a band of militants who were fighting for a separate state in northeast Sri Lanka (a country just south of India).

After her husband's assassination, Sonia Gandhi was devastated. She became a virtual recluse for the next six years, spending most of her time with her children and rarely leaving her home. She did break her silence twice. In 1992 Gandhi published a book called *Rajiv,* which offered an unexpected glimpse into the life she shared with her husband. In 1994 she went into more detail when she published *Rajiv's World.* She also preserved her husband's legacy by traveling throughout the world and establishing trust funds in his name. Remembering him in such ways provided at least some degree of healing.

Savior of the Congress Party

Throughout her seclusion, representatives from the Congress Party (CP) sent appeal after appeal to Gandhi asking her to be their leader. The CP, once the strongest party in India, had never recovered from Indira Gandhi's death, and by the 1990s it was in serious decline. At the same time, one of the opposition parties, the Bharatiya Janata Party (BJP), was fast gaining ground. Since most of India still revered the Gandhi name, representatives believed that Sonia Gandhi would offer the best hope of infusing new life into their party. Time and again Gandhi refused their offers. In 1997, however, realizing that the CP was in dire need, she agreed to formally join their ranks.

Although she had no political experience, Gandhi threw herself into the 1998 legislative campaign. She made more than 140 stops throughout the country, delivering speeches to packed audiences. And, even though she spoke in a very soft voice and in heavily accented Hindi, she touched the people of India. It may have been partly because she was seen as a grieving widow, or because voters saw her as a reminder of the party's past glory, but the CP was re-energized and Gandhi emerged as a political power in her own right. As one CP representative told CNN in December of 1998, "She gave the party again a nucleus around which it could get united."

Gandhi gained so much popularity that members of opposing parties, especially the BJP, saw her as a very real threat. In an attempt to undermine her credibility, they attacked her verbally and in the press, focusing on a single issue: Gandhi had no right to be involved in politics because, having been born in Italy, she was a foreigner. It did not seem to matter than Gandhi had become an Indian citizen in 1984. Such attacks did little harm, however, since most of the voting public did not consider Gandhi to be an outsider. As one male supporter told CNN in 1998, "Ever since she married Rajiv Gandhi, Sonia has lived in India. She has learned all about India and made herself an Indian. In fact, she is a good example of a good Indian woman."

Although the CP made a good showing in the 1998 elections, gaining twenty-eight seats in Parliament, the Bharatiya Janata Party came out the ultimate winner when it formed a coalition government with seventeen other lesser parties. Therefore, in March of 1998, BJP leader Atal Behari Vajpayee (1926–) was named prime minister. It was, however, a short-lived victory. Shaky to begin with, Vajpayee's government remained intact only until April of 1999, which meant that elections had to be held again in the fall of the year. In the meantime Gandhi was elected president of the CP, and it seemed possible that another Gandhi would soon be in the country's top position. Once again the question of Gandhi's right to be involved in politics came into play, although this time the outcry came from several top members of her own party. Not wishing to divide the group, Gandhi resigned. The CP refused to accept her resignation, however, and instead fired the members who had dared to oppose her.

When the October elections rolled around, it was still not clear whether Gandhi was the favored CP contender for prime minister. As it turned out, the point was not an issue, since the CP had a poor showing, capturing only 112 seats. The BJP claimed victory, with 182 seats, and Vajpayee once again formed a coalition government. Known as the National Democratic Alliance, the BJP-led government controlled almost three hundred of the 545 seats in the lower house of Parliament, the Lok Sabha. This time, Vajpayee managed to install a relatively stable coalition, and the BJP would remain in control for the next five years.

Took husband's seat in Parliament

In the same election Gandhi ran for two parliamentary positions, including the seat in Uttar Pradesh which Rajiv Gandhi had once held.

Supporters of Sonia Gandhi gather in front of her house in New Delhi, India, in 2004. AP/Wide World Photos. Reproduced by permission.

Candidates in India are allowed to run for two seats simultaneously; if they win both, they must choose which post to take. Gandhi ultimately won both seats, but chose the district her husband had represented.

Under BJP rule the country seemed to prosper, and by 2004 Vajpayee was claiming credit for turning the economy around. True, big business was booming and India was advancing technologically, but millions of rural Indians living in poverty were not benefiting from BJP reforms. According to statistics reported by CNN in 2004, half of the Indian population was living on less than two dollars a day. However, Vajpayee was so confident that voters were behind him that, although national elections were slated for October of 2004, he called for polls to open six months early.

Gandhi again hit the campaign trail, covering approximately forty thousand miles in the months prior to the elections, and spending long days speaking in sweltering heat that soared over one hundred degrees Fahrenheit. For most of her appearances she dressed in a simple white sari, which is the symbol of widowhood in India. She also spoke simply and plainly, and made a direct appeal to the nation's poor. In direct contrast to Vajpayee, who touted big business, Gandhi's campaign, according to Egbert Bhatty of the *Washington Dispatch,* focused on "unity, tolerance, and love among all men." As they had in 1998, millions of her countrymen embraced the soft-spoken Gandhi, calling her *desh ki bahu,* our daughter-in-law.

When elections began in April, voters turned out in droves. Almost four hundred million people went to the polls, and after all the ballots were counted in May, there was a surprise upset. The CP, along with its coalition allies, captured 279 seats, a slim majority, but a majority nonetheless, in the Lok Sabha. Since it had won a majority, the CP needed to elect a new prime minister, and the frontrunner seemed to be Sonia Gandhi. Although Gandhi remained tight-lipped about whether or not she wanted the position, political analysts predicted that her victory was assured, and CP members were vocal in their support. Elizabeth Roche of *The Age* quoted senior official Ambika Soni as saying, "Sonia Gandhi is the leader of the Congress party. We want that our party chief should become the prime minister."

The fairy tale ends?

On Tuesday, May 17, during a meeting of the CP, Gandhi made a declaration that stunned her party, the people of India, and the rest of the world. "I was always certain," she said, "that if ever I found myself in the position that I am in today, I would follow my inner voice. Today, that voice tells me that I must humbly decline this post." Gandhi's supporters pleaded with her to reconsider, but she remained firm in her decision to decline the position. Some claimed that she was bullied into her decision by the BJP opposition, who once again berated Gandhi because of her foreign birth. Others felt that she and her children feared for her safety. But the public Gandhi indicated that she was stepping aside for the good of her party and the good of India.

The day after her announcement, Gandhi nominated longtime friend and government official Manmohan Singh (1932–) to take the reigns as prime minister. On May 19, 2004, his appointment became official. Although Gandhi did not accept the country's top post, she remained at the helm of the CP, and those around her still considered her to be very much in the forefront of Indian politics. As Mani Shankar Aiyar of the CP told Bill Schneider of CNN.com, "She is the queen. She is appointing a regent to run some of the business of government for her. But it is she who will be in charge and who will continue to direct the fortunes of the Congress Party." In addition, after the 2004 elections, it seemed that the Gandhi dynasty would continue at least for another generation, since Sonia and Rajiv's son, Rahul, was successfully elected to the Indian Parliament.

For More Information

Periodicals

Omestad, Thomas. "The Ghandis Return." *U.S. News & World Report* (May 24, 2004): p. 14.

Walsh, James. "India: Death's Return Visit." *Time* (June 3, 1991).

Web Sites

Bhatty, Egbert F. "Sonia Gandhi: The Once and Future Prime Minister of India." *Washington Dispatch* (May 21, 2004). http://www.washington dispatch.com/printer_9110.shtml (accessed on July 5, 2004).

Bindra, Satinder. "Gandhi Dynasty Poised for Power." *CNN.com: World* (May 14, 2004). http://www.cnn.com/2004/WORLD/asiapcf/05/14/ india.vote1155/index.html (accessed on June 30, 2004).

Gandhi, Sonia. Speech, Congress Parliamentary Party meeting (New Delhi, India, May 17, 2004). *rediff.com.* http://in.rediff.com/election/2004/ may/18sonia2.htm (accessed on July 5, 2004).

Haidar, Suhasini, and Ram Ramgopal. "Singh: Poster Boy of Change." *CNN.com: World* (May 20, 2004). http://www.cnn.com/2004/WORLD/ asiapcf/05/20/india.singh/index.html (accessed on July 5, 2004).

Pratap, Anita. "An Enigmatic Sonia Gandhi Transforms Indian Politics." *CNN.com: World* (December 12, 1998). http://www.cnn.com/WORLD/asiapcf/9812/12/india.sonia.gandhi/index.html (accessed on June 29, 2004).

"Profile: Sonia Gandhi." *BBC News: World Edition* (May 14, 2004). http://news.bbc.co.uk/2/hi/south_asia/3546851.stm (accessed on June 29, 2004).

Roche, Elizabeth. "Sonia Gandhi Tightens Grip on Presidency." *The Age.com* (May 15, 2004). http://www.theage.com.au/articles/2004/05/15/1084570991729.html?from=storylhs&oneclick=true# (accessed on June 30, 2004).

Schneider, Bill. "Gandhi Has Power, but Declines Post." *CNN.com: Inside Politics* (May 21, 2004). http://www.cnn.com/2004/ALLPOLITICS/05/21/gandhi/index.html (accessed on July 5, 2004).

Fond of fish

Frank Gehry was born Ephraim Goldberg on February 28, 1929, in Toronto, Ontario, Canada. He and his sister, Doreen, were raised in Timmins, a small mining town in eastern Ontario, by the extended Goldberg family. Father Irving was a former boxer who traveled selling pinball and slot machines. Sometimes Gehry would make sales calls with his father, which meant that he made frequent stops at bars at a very young age. In a *Smithsonian* magazine profile, he was quick to point out, "But my mother took me to concerts and introduced me to art, so there was a balance."

> "I'm only an architect, no matter what anybody says—a humble architect."

Gehry also considers his grandmother to be an early influence. He fondly remembers building imaginary cities with her using woodshavings scavenged from his grandfather's hardware store. He also remembers the carp that his grandmother let swim around in the family bathtub on Friday nights. The Goldbergs were Jewish and gefilte fish, a seasoned ground fish dish, was a favorite for Sabbath, or Saturday night, dinner. In later years Gehry regularly used fish motifs in many of his designs. "I never intended to build fish," Gehry told Kurt Andersen of *Time*. "In my mind, I say 'Enough with the fish.' But it has a life of its own."

By the mid-1940s the family was experiencing hardships on several fronts. Following World War II (1939–45) the Canadian government began cracking down on gambling and Irving Goldberg's business suffered. At the same time the family lost most of their savings as a result of some bad investments. Then, in 1947, Goldberg suffered a heart attack, which was severe enough that his doctor suggested a change of scenery to help him recuperate. As a result, the entire family left Canada for Los Angeles, California. Gehry had just graduated from high school, and the move proved to be an important one. He has lived the rest of his life in California, and critics considered him to be very much a California designer—brash, bold, and unpretentious.

Breaks from the modernist mold

Gehry took a job as a truck driver in order to pay for night-school art classes and eventually enrolled in the school of architecture at the University of Southern California (USC). He was inspired to get a degree in architecture by one of his teachers who invited him to visit a construction site. "I was quite moved by watching the architect walking around, supervising, by the things he was worried about," Gehry recalled to Patrick Rogers of *People* magazine. In 1952 Gehry married his first wife, a stenographer who helped put him through school. The two were married for sixteen years and had two daughters, Brina and Leslie. According to Gehry his wife encouraged him to change his name. Gehry was taunted and beaten up when he was a boy in Toronto because he was Jewish, and his wife feared the same for their children. He now regrets his decision. "I wouldn't do it today," Gehry told Rogers.

After graduating from USC in 1954, Gehry had a one-year stint in the U.S. Army, Special Services Division. It was during this time that he began experimenting with furniture design since his assignment was to make furniture for the enlisted soldiers. Gehry's designs were so good that his tables and chairs usually ended up in the officers' quarters. He then spent a year studying city planning at the Harvard Graduate School of Design, in Cambridge, Massachusetts. In 1957 Gehry returned to California and worked for several years with established architecture firms, before opening his own design firm in 1962.

Gehry's early projects were fairly typical of the times and followed the modernist style. Modernist architecture stressed clean, geometric lines, with no clutter and no decoration. Simplicity was key; functionality was the focus. Gehry the artist, however, was itching to experiment. He was very much caught up in the West Coast art movement and counted many emerging artists as his friends, including Ed Moses (1936–) and Billy Al Bengston (1934–). By the mid-1960s, Gehry started to, as Richard Lacayo of *Time* put it, "insinuate odd bits of business into his designs." He began using materials such as unpainted plywood, rough concrete, and corrugated metal, all of which are usually hidden after a house is "properly finished." As Gehry told Lacayo, "I was trying to humanize stuff."

Icon or eyesore

In 1972 Gehry had his first flirtation with celebrity, not for his architecture, but for a line of furniture made out of layers of corrugated cardboard. Again, Gehry was experimenting with the traditional functions of materials, since cardboard was not usually considered in furniture design. Called Easy Edges, the chairs and tables were lightweight, inexpensive, and fun. Gehry pulled the plug on the project three months into production, claiming he did not want to be tied down by making mass-produced furniture. In the late 1970s he introduced Experimental Edges, a more upscale version of Easy Edges. According to Gehry, the reason he dabbles in furniture design and other small projects is because he gets a "quick fix." "Architecture takes so long," he told Jennifer Barrett of *Newsweek*. "That's why you do the small stuff—instant gratification."

Gehry undertook a steady stream of business during this period, designing private homes and small public buildings, mostly in California. It was the renovation of his own home in Santa Monica, however, that brought him back into the spotlight. What started out as a simple 1920s pink bungalow turned into what Kurt Andersen described as an "unfinished looking structure from a new-wave Oz." Gehry left the pink exterior of his home intact, but encased it in a shell made from metal, chain-link fencing, and glass. As he explained to *Smithsonian,* his intention was to "build a new house around the old and try to maintain a tension between the two, by having the one define the other." The bizarre structure caused quite a tension between Gehry and his neighbors, who threatened to take him to court because they considered it an eyesore.

Gehry's once-quiet street became a mecca for architecture students who came from all over the world to see the elaborate pink concoction. Gehry also received a lot of national attention, although not all of it positive. Many of his corporate clients were turned off by the experimental building, and several pulled their contracts. His large-scale business may have suffered, but private clients who commissioned Gehry to renovate studios and homes were more than happy to work with the innovative architect who coined the term *cheapscape* to describe his style of working with inexpensive, man-made materials. And museum directors, such as Richard Koshalek, head of the Los Angeles Museum of Contemporary Art (MOCA), praised him for his vision. Gehry designed a gallery for the MOCA in 1982 that incorporated a chain-link canopy over the street. The gallery was in an industrial section of Los Angeles, and according to Gehry, as quoted by *Smithsonian,* it "established a territory, and gave the building substance from the outside." In the same article, Koshalek responded, "Frank understands space; many architects don't.... He uses common materials like an artist, with elegance."

From bad boy to innovator

Exhilarated by his newfound freedom, Gehry decided that the edge was where he wanted to be, and he started over from scratch. He reduced his office staff from thirty to three and resolved to take on only work that he truly wanted to do. This led to international commissions including the Fishdance Restaurant (1986) in Kobe, Japan, and the Vitra Design Museum (1987) in Germany, and, of course, to several projects based in his native California, such as the California Aerospace Museum in Los Angeles (1982). The museum houses a collection of planes and exhibits and is composed of several different structural shapes, including a metal polygon and a stucco cube. On the front, poised just over the entrance, Gehry attached a F104 Starfighter jet. The jet serves as an immediate "billboard" advertising the function of the building to passersby.

In 1987 Gehry was honored with a retrospective of his works by the Walker Art Center in Minneapolis, Minnesota, and by the late 1980s critics were recognizing him as more than just an eccentric California architect. As Kurt Andersen wrote, "He may no longer be written off as an idiosyncratic California bad boy. He must be regarded as one of the two or three more important members of the late-modernist generation—and maybe the most successful innovator of them all." In 1989 Gehry's peers agreed and awarded him the Pritzker Architecture Prize, the most prestigious honor that can be given to a living architect.

The late 1980s also saw Gehry turning to technology to solve some of his elaborate design problems. Although he begins by physically creating three-dimensional models, sometimes using crumpled paper and soda bottles for the very early ones, computers are necessary to plot out the complicated design specs. Gehry's computer program was adapted from software used in the manufacture of Boeing jets. A decade later, it proved key in designing what became Gehry's most famous building, the Guggenheim Museum in Bilbao, Spain. With its swooping titanium arches and jutting wings, it looks like something poised to take flight. Master architect Philip Johnson (1906–), as quoted by Richard Lacayo, proclaimed it to be the "most important building of our time."

The public was also intrigued by Gehry's modern marvel. The Guggenheim, which opened in 1997, drew more than a million visitors its first year, and suddenly Bilbao, a city that was previously unremarkable, became a tourist haven. As Lacayo noted, Gehry "managed to be both intellectually respectable and popular."

The Walt Disney Concert Hall

After his Guggenheim triumph, Gehry worked harder than ever, both in the United States and around the world. For example, in 1999 he finished the aluminum-covered office complex known as the Frank O. Gehry buildings, in Dusseldorf, Germany. A year later, he unveiled the Music Experience Project in Seattle, Washington, a $100 million interactive rock and roll museum. Gehry returned to Los Angeles, however, to create what many claim is a masterpiece to rival the Guggenheim, the Walt Disney Concert Hall.

The project had been in the works since 1987 when Lillian Disney (1899–1997), widow of American icon Walt Disney (1901–1966), decided to build a new hall to house the Los Angeles Philharmonic. The following year Gehry won the competition to design the hall, which was surprising at the time since he was still known as the weird architect who used chain-link fencing. When faced with his modern, spiraling designs, the ninety-year-old Disney was perplexed. Gehry won her over by showing her the inspiration for his design—a single white rose floating in a bowl of water.

Work on the hall went in fits and starts, stalled over the years by earthquakes, riots, and a lack of funds. In 1997 Lillian Disney died, and many thought perhaps her dream died with her. That same year, however, the Guggenheim opened and Gehry's instant star status infused new life into the proposal. Funding came through, and fifteen years after he began, Gehry unveiled the finished hall in October of 2003. The structure looks like a cascade of shiny, metal ribbon unfurled against the sky.

In *Time* magazine, Gehry called it "a boat where the wind is behind you." It is especially unique because Gehry seems to have captured the essence of the hall's namesake. As Richard Lacayo pointed out, the shining arcs bring to mind the magic wand of Disney dancing in the air.

The Walt Disney Concert Hall, designed by Frank Gehry. © Ted Soqui/Corbis.

For the curving interior Gehry used Douglas fir to create comfortable, cozy surroundings for concert-goers, who are also treated to floral-patterned cushioned seats. The seat design is a tribute to Lillian Disney. In addition, since functionality is so central, Gehry wanted the musicians to be happy. He worked closely with a Japanese acoustics company to ensure that his design would provide a perfect harmonious setting. One day while the orchestra was practicing, Gehry was in the audience. "One of the bass players looked at me," he recounted to Lacayo, "and gave me this big thumbs up. That's when I knew it was all O.K."

The future is Gehry

With the Disney Hall, Gehry transformed the skyline of Los Angeles, just as he had done in Bilbao, and so changed the face of those cities forever. He also shook up the world of architecture, again. According to Lacayo, "[The Disney Hall] can be counted on to reverberate not just through L.A. but across the U.S., raising the stakes everywhere for what a building can be." Gehry continues to raise those stakes since his design calendar is booked solid for some time. He was seventy-four when the Disney Hall opened, but there are plans in the pipeline for a new theater in Brooklyn, New York, a hospital wing in Scotland, and a museum extension in Toronto. In addition, Gehry still works on the smaller stuff: designing watches for Fossil and a new SuperLight chair made from aluminum that weighs only 6 pounds.

Gehry and his second wife, Berta, who serves as chief financial officer (CFO) of his design firm, live in the same house that the California architect transformed back in the 1970s. And Gehry still runs his studio, which has now grown to over 140 employees. In his spare time, the rumpled, soft-spoken artist enjoys sailing in the Santa Monica Bay and playing ice hockey. He took up the sport at age sixty. Looking ahead, he would like to become involved in urban renewal projects in Los Angeles and New York. "I'm not going to retire," Gehry told *People* magazine, "I'll just keep going."

For More Information

Books

Gehry, Frank. *Symphony: Frank Gehry's Walt Disney Concert Hall*. New York: Harry Abrams, 2003.

Periodicals

Andersen, Kurt. "Building Beauty the Hard Way: After Years of Risky Experience, Frank Gehry Relaxes." *Time* (October 13, 1986).

Lacayo, Richard. "The Art of Warp." *Time* (October 27, 2003): p. 71.

Lacayo, Richard. "The Frank Gehry Experience." *Time* (June 26, 2000): pp. 64–68.

Rogers, Patrick. "Dream Builder: Architect Frank Gehry Creates Tomorrow's Fanciful Landmarks." *People Weekly* (July 10, 2000): pp. 114–115.

Webb, Michael. "A Man Who Made Architecture the Art of the Unexpected." *Smithsonian* (April 1987): p. 48.

Web Sites

"Architect: Frank Gehry." *Great Buildings Online*. http://www.great buildings.com/architects/Frank_Gehry.html (accessed August 1, 2004).

Barrett, Jennifer. "Frank Gehry Has Designed Everything from Cardboard Chairs to Vodka Bottles. His Next Project: Remaking New York City." *MSNBC News: Newsweek* (April 16, 2004). http://msnbc.msn.com/id/4759758/site/newsweek (accessed August 1, 2004).

"Frank Gehry, Pritzker Architecture Prize Laureate: 1989." *Pritzker Prize Web site*. http://www.pritzkerprize.com/gehry.htm (accessed August 1, 2004).

Julie Gerberding

August 22, 1955 • *Estelline, South Dakota*

Director, Centers for Disease Control and Prevention

AP/Wide World Photos. Reproduced by permission.

Julie Gerberding is a physician and an expert in infectious diseases. As director of the Centers for Disease Control and Prevention (CDC), she also holds what may be the most important medical job in the United States since the CDC is the federal agency in charge of protecting the health and safety of the American public. That task has been a challenge since Gerberding took on the job of director in July of 2002. Before she could settle into her position, she was confronted with the mysterious viral infection known as severe acute respiratory syndrome (SARS). That epidemic was followed by an outbreak of the rare monkeypox virus, and an especially widespread threat of the West Nile virus. In addition, as head of the CDC, it is up to Gerberding to make sure that the American health system is prepared to handle a bioterrorist strike, a very real threat since the attacks of September 11, 2001. Gerberding, the first woman to hold the post of CDC director, remains undaunted. In 2004 she announced a massive reorganization and vowed in *Time* magazine that she is "redefining [the] CDC as the nation's health-protection agency."

A born physician

Julie Louise Gerberding was born on August 22, 1955, in Estelline, a tiny rural town in South Dakota, where her father was the police chief and her mother was a schoolteacher. Gerberding knew from the very beginning that she wanted to be a doctor. In fact, she built her first laboratory to study the life cycle of bugs in her parents' basement. After high school, Gerberding moved to Cleveland, Ohio, to attend Case

"There is no time to lose. Our waistlines are expanding while our health is deteriorating."

Western Reserve University. While an undergraduate she received the school's top science prizes, and in 1977, she earned a bachelor's degree in chemistry and biology, graduating with honors. After some consideration, Gerberding decided to stay at Case to pursue her medical degree. She graduated in 1981, again with high honors. Gerberding also took home Case Western's Alice Paige Cleveland Prize, which is awarded to a woman graduate who displays outstanding leadership qualities.

Gerberding headed to the West Coast to complete her internship and residency training at the University of California, San Francisco (UCSF). This was in the early 1980s, and San Francisco was being hit hard by an unknown disease; as a result, the young physician became involved in the early battle against acquired immunodeficiency syndrome (AIDS). As Gerberding explained in a 2003 *CWRU* interview, "My clinical training really evolved with the AIDS epidemic and it was natural for me to get started in the infectious disease area during that time." She completed a fellowship in pharmacology (the study of drugs and their effects) and infectious diseases, and in 1990 was named director of UCSF's Epidemiology Prevention and Interventions (EPI) Center. Epidemiology is the area of medicine that deals with the control and transmission of disease.

VERB: It's What You Do

The issue of obesity is not a uniquely American one. In 2004 the World Health Organization estimated that over one billion adults worldwide were overweight, which put them at risk of such diseases as diabetes, cancer, and heart attack. In May of 2004, Julie Gerberding represented the CDC at an international conference in Geneva, Switzerland. The United States, along with 194 other countries, met to approve the Global Strategy on Diet, Physical Activity and Health, which recommends that people change their diets and habits by exercising more and limiting their intake of fat, salt, and sugar.

At home, the CDC put the recommendation into action by launching a $190 million national multicultural campaign called VERB: It's What You Do. According to the program's Web site, the goal is to help preteens and teens get active in a "cool and meaningful way." CDC statistics point to the fact that 30 percent of children watch at least five hours of television a day. VERB offers tools and tips for parents to help get the family off the couch and on the go. One idea is for families to explore sports from other countries. For example, broomball, which originated in Canada in the 1900s, is similar to hockey; it is played on ice, but instead of hockey pucks and sticks, players use brooms and balls.

At the Web site there are quizzes, polls, and incentives to track activity hours, like a chance to win sports gear from the Women's National Basketball Association (WNBA). There are also activity suggestions for almost every day of the year, including a Bike to School Day or have a race with Mom on Mother's Day.

Gerberding and her colleagues at the EPI were instrumental in creating guidelines to help prevent the transmission of AIDS to healthcare workers. They also developed a medical procedure to combat infection in workers who had been exposed through needles. In addition, the EPI became an information center for businesses about how to deal with people infected with HIV in the workplace. Gerberding quickly became known in the medical community as an authority on AIDS and she continues to be a leading advocate to this day at the CDC. As she commented to Lois Bowers of *CWRU:* "AIDS is the number one health problem affecting most of the developing world as well as the developed world. It is an agency priority that we do our share of interventions to prevent its spread."

Stays calm during anthrax scare

In 1998 Gerberding went to work for the Centers for Disease Control and Prevention (CDC), a federal agency that is part of the Department of Health and Human Services. Established in 1946, the mission of the

CDC, as stated on its Web site, is "to promote health and quality of life by preventing and controlling disease, injury, and disability." The agency carries out this mission by partnering with other groups both in the United States and abroad to, according to the CDC Web site, "detect and investigate health problems; conduct research to enhance prevention; develop and advocate sound public health policies; implement prevention strategies; promote healthy behaviors; foster safe and healthful environments; and provide leadership and training." Over eight thousand people are employed by the CDC, which is based in Atlanta, Georgia. The CDC is composed of twelve operational units, or offices, including the National Center for Environmental Health and the National Center for Infectious Diseases (NCID).

When Gerberding joined the CDC, she became the director of the Division of Healthcare Quality Promotion, which is part of the NCID. She used her expertise to further research into the area of hospital safety, and focused specifically on investigating medical errors and drug-resistant infections. Just three years later, in 2001, Gerberding was appointed acting director of the NCID. Almost immediately she was faced with a national emergency. Just one month after the terrorist attacks of September 11, 2001, there were several reports of anthrax, a potentially fatal disease of the lungs, in Florida and Washington, D.C. Experts suspected foul play since anthrax is usually transmitted to humans by contaminated animals. The NCID instantly went to work, and together with other federal agencies and local health organizations, discovered letters containing anthrax spores in District of Columbia postal facilities and various news organizations. A widespread panic spread across the country, and people became wary of opening their mail.

As the NCID spokesperson, it was Gerberding's job to address the public and many credit her for calming a frightened nation. She appeared confident in press conferences, and she explained the complicated situation in clear, concise terms. Even after the scare, bioterrorism (deliberate attacks using germ warfare) remained a key health concern. In a 2002 CDC press release, Gerberding reassured the public that measures were being taken to ensure their safety: "CDC's response to the anthrax attacks required input from experts throughout the agency and they were there. We have the people, we have the plans and now we have the practice. We're building our knowledge

and capacity every day to assure that CDC and our partners are ready to respond to any terrorist event."

Dr. Julie Gerberding, director of the CDC, speaks during a 2003 press conference on Severe Acute Respiratory Syndrome (SARS). AP/Wide World Photos. Reproduced by permission.

SARS, monkeypox, and West Nile

In spring of 2002, when CDC director Jeffrey Koplan announced that he was stepping down, it came as no surprise that Gerberding was being considered for the job. Tommy Thompson (1941–), the Secretary of Health and Human Services, especially championed her appointment, and when the official call came through in July, it was Thompson who spoke to the press. "I can think of no one better equipped to take the helm," he said, as quoted on CNN.com. "[Gerberding] brings the right mix of professional experience and leadership skills to ensure the CDC continues to meet the nation's public health needs."

Barely six months in the director's chair, Gerberding's skills were put to the test when the United States once again faced a mysterious illness. This time it was labeled severe acute respiratory syndrome, or SARS. Although the disease originated in Asia, with China hit particularly hard, it soon became apparent that this was a disease that traveled. By May of 2003, there were almost seven thousand cases reported in almost thirty countries. Although only approximately sixty of the cases appeared in the United States, people were frightened because the flu-like disease was potentially fatal. Gerberding and the CDC worked quickly to join with international researchers in understanding what caused the virus and how it was spread. And, again, Julie Gerberding was the voice of reason for the American public.

Throughout 2003, Gerberding appeared regularly in the press, providing statistical updates and fielding countless questions. She answered honestly and clearly, explaining that the disease was spread through face-to-face contact, specifically through droplets spread by a cough or sneeze. She admitted that it was a sobering situation, but she also warned that it was difficult to separate the "help from the hype." In a press conference on April 14, 2003, she offered some simple precautionary steps: "My advice is to kind of follow the same rules that your mother taught you in kindergarten. Keep your hands clean, and cover your mouth with a tissue if you're coughing and sneezing. And use common sense."

Just as the press over SARS started to die down, other national health concerns dominated the headlines during the summer of 2003, including a rare outbreak of monkeypox in the Midwest and a return of the West Nile virus. The monkeypox virus is usually isolated to Africa, but in June there were more than sixty cases reported in the United States. The CDC was called in and quickly linked the infection to prairie dogs, intended for sale as pets, which had been bitten by an infected African rat. As a result the CDC launched an investigation into the exotic pet trade. An ongoing issue was the West Nile virus, a disease that is spread primarily through mosquito bites. Because of heavy rainfall in the Eastern United States, there was a rash of cases. According to CDC reports, in 2003 West Nile infected 9,862 Americans, 264 of whom died.

Everyday challenges

Although rare diseases and bioterrorism tended to grab the spotlight, Gerberding stressed that the CDC remained committed to public health concerns that are ongoing. As she noted to Lois Bowers of *CWRU*, "The CDC ... exists to promote safe, healthier people in all communities, and those priorities have not changed at all since 9/11." In 2003 the agency's annual budget increased to $7.2 billion. This would allow the CDC to focus its energies on such chronic issues as diabetes, asthma, and obesity. In 2004 the agency paid particular attention to the issue of weight control. According to CDC statistics cited by Kim Severson of the *San Francisco Chronicle*, "deaths related to poor diet and too little exercise have increased by 33 percent over the last decade." The agency predicted that if the trend continued, being overweight and out of shape would soon become the number-one cause of preventable death in the United States.

In 2004 Gerberding was also committed to restructuring the CDC, which she claimed was like a jigsaw puzzle when she first came on board. In an effort to streamline processes, the number of directors reporting to Gerberding was reduced from twenty-five to thirteen and the various units were grouped under four centers. On May 13, 2004, Gerberding announced that the agency would focus on two major health protection goals: Preparedness, which will ensure that each person in every community is protected from infectious, environmental, and terrorist threats; and Health Promotion and Prevention of Disease, Injury, and Disability, with a special focus on improving the quality of health at "every stage of life." Gerberding acknowledged that the CDC was an "extraordinary agency with the greatest workforce in the world," but she also observed that "today's world characterized by tremendous globalization, connectivity, and speed poses entirely new challenges. The steps we are taking through this initiative will better position us to meet these challenges head on."

With Gerberding at the helm, the CDC should be able to meet almost any challenge. A dedicated caregiver, a natural leader, and a gifted researcher, she is active on many fronts outside of the agency despite her often grueling schedule. In addition to being a wife and mother, Gerberding is an associate professor of medicine at Emory University in Atlanta, and belongs to a number of professional organizations, including the American Society for Clinical Investigation. She also serves as an adviser to several health organizations, one of which is the newly formed Grand Challenges in Global Health Initiative. The goal of the organization, which is composed of experts in a variety of health fields, is to come up with the key issues that need to be addressed in order to effect change at a global level. Gerberding, still sounding like the young doctor who was a pioneer in the 1980s, told *CWRU,* "We're going to be thinking out of the box, we're going to be thinking big, and we're going to be thinking, 'What can we do that will have the most impact?'"

For More Information

Periodicals

Bowers, Lois A. "The Front Line: Julie Gerberding." *CWRU Magazine* (spring 2003): pp. 29–31.

Park, Alice. "Julie Gerberding: The Health-Crisis Manager." *Time* (April 26, 2004): p. 102.

Severson, Kim. "Weighty Crusade: Worldwide Efforts Promote Healthier Diets, More Exercise." *San Francisco Chronicle* (May 23, 2004): p. A1.

Web Sites

"As Americans Reflect on 9/11, HHS and CDC Continue to Aggressively Prepare the Nation for Another Terrorist Attack." *Centers for Disease Control and Prevention,* Office of Communication. (September 9, 2002). http://www.cdc.gov/od/oc/media/pressrel/r020909.htm (accessed August 1, 2004).

"CDC Announces New Goals and Organizational Design." *Centers for Disease Control and Prevention,* Office of Communication (May 13, 2004). http://www.cdc.gov/od/oc/media/pressrel/r040513.htm (accessed August 1, 2004).

"CDC Chief on Public Health's Front Line." *CNN.com: World News* (April 19, 2004). http://www.cnn.com/2004/WORLD/americas/04/16/gerberd ing (accessed August 1, 2004).

Centers for Disease Control and Prevention Web site. http://www.cdc.gov (accessed August 1, 2004).

"SARS: Genetic Sequencing of Coronavirus." *Centers for Disease Control and Prevention,* Office of Communication (April 14, 2003). http://www.cdc.gov/od/oc/media/transcripts/t030414.htm (accessed August 1, 2004).

VERB Now.com! Centers for Disease Control and Prevention. http://www.verbnow.com (accessed August 1, 2004).

"WHO's Anti-Obesity Plan Wins Backing from U.S., Food Industry." *Bloomberg.com: News & Commentary* (May 20, 2004). http://quote.bloomberg.com/apps/news?pid=10000103&sid=aAmoQey1ZIBc&refe r=us (accessed August 1, 2004).

Brian Graden

Photo by Keith Bedford/Getty Images.

March 23, 1963 • *Hillsboro, Illinois*

President of programming, MTV and VH1

Brian Graden has the knack—the knack for knowing what twenty-year-olds want to watch when they grab the remote control. As president of entertainment for MTV and VH1, Graden is responsible for deciding which programs will be the next big hits and which ones are destined to fizzle. Although the network uses market research to gauge viewer likes and dislikes, success often comes down to instinct. It is that instinct that prompted Graden to introduce original, reality programs to MTV, which transformed it from a music-video cable network to a mega-hit, must-watch channel. In 2002 Graden was charged with refreshing the identity of MTV's sister network VH1, a channel aimed at Generation X (people born in the 1960s and 1970s). VH1 soared in the ratings, and Graden proved again that he could tap into any audience. As MTV president Judy McGrath told *Broadcasting & Cable,* "Everything Brian does breaks through and yet is completely in touch with the popular culture."

Not cut out for finance

Brian Graden has always been obsessed with music and television. He was born on March 23, 1963, in the rural community of Hillsboro, Illinois, population five thousand. When he was young, Graden taught himself how to play the piano, and by the time he was a teenager he was a major rock-music fan. In high school he and his friends formed a cover band called Ace Oxygen and the Ozones, with Graden on keyboards. When not practicing he and the band spent a lot of their time watching a brand new channel on television that showed only videos. This was Graden's first taste of MTV. As he recalled to Jeffrey Epstein of *The Advocate,* "I was 16 or 17 when MTV first came on the

> **"You can never become static. It is more fun to move on to something new, something you haven't tried before."**

scene. Nobody had cable, but there was one person in the whole city who had satellite. So we would go over to his basement and just watch for hours and hours."

When Graden was eighteen the future of the Ozones was threatened when the guitar player's father, who was a minister, found out that his son was playing in bars. As a result, he shipped his son off to the ultra-conservative Oral Roberts University, in Tulsa, Oklahoma. The determined bandmates followed, but the reunion was short-lived as the Ozones broke up just a few years later. Since his future as a rock musician seemed doubtful, Graden wondered about his next move. After graduating from Oral Roberts in 1985, he headed to Harvard University, in Cambridge, Massachusetts, to study business, still not sure where it would lead. One glimpse into his future came in 1988 when he took the summer off to intern at the newly formed Fox network.

With graduation approaching, and resume in hand, Graden made the usual round of calls to interview for a job. After going from one Wall Street firm to another, it started to become clear that high finance

MTV: A Network with a Conscience

MTV is known for videos and for outrageous reality shows like *Punk'd,* where each week Hollywood heartthrob Ashton Kutcher (1978–) plays another wacky prank on one of his celebrity pals. But, since Brian Graden took the helm of the network in the late 1990s, it has also become known as a platform for raising social awareness. Graden, who is openly gay, made a special point of using public-service messages, documentaries, and regular programming to teach tolerance. "[MTV] is not pro-anything," he told *The Advocate,* "except tolerance. We believe that everyone should have a chance to be heard, and it's hard to argue with that."

One particularly powerful campaign, called Fight for Your Rights: Take a Stand against Discrimination, was launched in 2001. MTV kicked off the campaign by airing *Anatomy of a Hate Crime,* an original docudrama about Matthew Shepard, a young gay college student who was brutally murdered in 1998. The movie debuted without commercials, and immediately following, MTV ceased its regular programming for seventeen hours; instead the network continuously scrolled the names of hate-crime victims along the bottom of the screen. Graden claims that there was no debate about the decision. "When the idea came up," he explained to *Philadelphia Weekly,* "we just went ahead and did it because that's the kind of thing we should be doing."

In 2002 Graden was awarded the Tom Stoddard National Role Model Award, an annual award given by the Equality Forum to people or institutions that, according to *Philadelphia Weekly,* "promote greater understanding and sensitivity to gay and lesbian issues." According to a representative of the organization, "We believe that there is no single entity that has a greater impact [than TV] on shaping the attitudes of young people about gays and lesbians." Graden credits MTV for being open to the issues and claims that this is one reason he stays where he is. As he told *The Advocate,* "As a television executive, I could work anywhere, but I wanted to be here because MTV is a network that wants to do more than entertain."

was not for him. During one interview, in particular, it became crystal clear. In several magazine articles, Graden described his moment of revelation when an executive at a potential employer asked him: "Why do you want to be me? Why do you want my job?" His immediate response, as he told Allison Romano of *Broadcasting & Cable,* was "I can't imagine anything more horrifying than being you."

The programming czar

In 1989, following graduation from Harvard, Graden moved to Los Angeles, California, hoping to get hired at Fox. He ended up working on the network's production staff, and just four years later, in 1993, he became vice president for program development. He also headed up

Foxlab, a branch of the network that was in charge of alternative programming. Graden and his Foxlab creative team were responsible for launching such reality shows as *America's Most Wanted* and *Cops*. Always on the lookout for new talent, it was during this time that Graden happened upon two young writers who had just made their first live-action film, called *Cannibal the Musical* (1994). Their names were Trey Parker (1969–) and Matt Stone (1971–), and little did Graden know that the three would soon make television history. Graden hired Parker and Stone to create a Christmas video card for him to send out to friends, which resulted in *The Spirit of Christmas*, a five-minute animated short that eventually gave birth to *South Park*.

The video created such a buzz that Graden quickly tried to hire Parker and Stone to create a regular series. Fox, however, decided to pass on the project, a decision that prompted Graden to leave the network. "If Fox was not the kind of culture where South Park could be accommodated," he remarked to Romano, "then I questioned whether broadcast was the kind of medium where ideas could be accommodated." Graden left Fox and moved with Parker and Stone to the cable network Comedy Central, which first aired *South Park* in August of 1997. The irreverent animated series was an immediate hit, just the first example of the Graden development magic in action.

Shortly before *South Park* debuted, Graden left Comedy Central to branch out with his own production company. Before he had a chance, however, he was approached by a recruiter who was hiring for MTV. Graden did not think twice about abandoning his fledgling company; this was his childhood dream come true. This was not, however, the MTV that Graden grew up with. When MTV was launched in 1981, it was a revolutionary concept—a cable channel targeted at teenagers that aired nothing but music videos twenty-four-hours a day. It was basically televised radio, complete with veejays who introduced the music clips. By the 1990s, viewers were demanding more than just music videos, and MTV began featuring more and more non-music programming, some of it animated like *Beavis and Butthead,* and some of it reality-based, such as *The Real World.*

He was at the network less than four months when Graden was named executive vice president in charge of programming, or as his boss Judy McGrath put it, he became the "programming czar." Graden was tasked with revamping the MTV lineup, which was causing the network to slip dangerously in the ratings. Others at MTV assumed that Graden would cut back on the non-music programming, but he had other plans. As he told *Variety* in 1997, "the real idea here is to find ideas that cut through and get people's attention." And get their attention he did. Graden expanded the definition of reality TV by pushing forward prank-based comedy programs such as *The Tom Green Show,* featuring quirky Canadian funnyman Tom Green (1972–). And in 1998, he championed interactive television when he gave the thumbs up to *Total Request Live,* a call-in video request show that remains an MTV staple.

Behind the scenes at MTV

MTV ratings steadily rose and Graden developed a reputation for having his finger on the pulse of the young, hip market. In 2000 he was promoted to president of programming for MTV, as well as companion channel MTV2. "I was completely overwhelmed," Graden admitted to *The Advocate,* "but this was the moment I'd been waiting for." His success was only beginning. In spring 2002 Graden hit the jackpot when he launched *The Osbournes,* a program that followed the daily lives of bad-boy rock legend Ozzy Osbourne (1948–) and his family, including wife Sharon and children Jack and Kelly. Again, Graden had created another kind of reality show, this time blending music, the backbone of MTV, and a behind-the-scenes look at celebrity life. The show became an enormous hit, drawing millions of fans each week, and the Osbournes became America's favorite dysfunctional family.

Since viewers were only too eager to get a glimpse into the lives of the famous and nearly famous, Graden cashed in with similar series, including *Newlyweds: Nick and Jessica,* which chronicled the ups and downs of newly married pop singers Jessica Simpson (1980–) and Nick Lachey (1973–). When the program premiered in August of 2003, Simpson and Lachey were blips on the music scene: Simpson was considered a pretty blonde clone; Lachey was a member of minor boy band 98 degrees. By the end of 2003, after they opened the doors of their Beverly Hills mansion for the cameras, they were the hottest couple in Hollywood. When *Newlyweds* began its second season on January 21, 2004, it was seen by 4.7 million viewers and was the number-one show in its time slot.

While MTV was enjoying an upswing, VH1 was nosediving. Formed in 1986 as an MTV alternative for a more mature audience, the channel focused on the lighter side of pop music. It did not enjoy real success, however, until the 1990s when, like MTV, it began to supplement its video format with music-related shows. The network hit it big with programs like *Pop-Up Video,* a novelty show where quick information clips "popped up" during videos, and *Behind the Music,* which profiled the lives of the music industry's biggest stars. Unfortunately, as Megan Larson of *Mediaweek* put it, the programs "suffered death by overplay." Instead of building its lineup, the network looped the same programs over and over, day after day. As a result, viewers got bored and tuned out. Enter Brian Graden.

Brian Graden poses with Carmen Electra and Dave Navarro, who appeared on MTV's reality show From Death Do Us Part *(2004).* Kevin Mazur/WireImage.com.

A nostalgia kick at VH1

In early 2002 management tapped Graden to become president of programming for VH1, hoping that he could resurrect the network just as he had done with MTV. Insiders wondered if being in charge of two networks would spread even a dynamo like Graden too thin. Graden, however, was not worried. As he told Allison Romano, "In my own journey, I was ready for a new puzzle." But, after spending some time in the VH1 offices and examining the situation, he had some doubts. First of all, VH1 staffers did not work in the same electric environment that existed at MTV. And, second, Graden discovered that there was actually very little development going on. As he told Larson, "I looked in the cupboard and saw three or four things that had some life. Virtual panic set in."

Graden immediately set about revving up the staff. At meetings he encouraged everyone, from researchers to writers to graphic artists, to express themselves. His one rule, as he explained to *Mediaweek* was "don't trash anyone's idea." Soon the energy level at the network had kicked into high gear and even the look and feel of on-air programming was recharged. Graphics and program promotions became hip and edgy, reflecting the tastes of the VH1 Gen-X audience. By the second half of 2002, ratings were up by 50 percent, and it looked like

VH1 was on the rebound. Some critics, however, had their doubts, claiming that Graden was offering some quick fixes, but little new content. "[He] applied some great band-aids to get them to the next step," a Starcom Entertainment director told *Mediaweek*. "We have not seen a real daringness in programming yet."

Graden was just getting started. Again, he put out his feelers and tapped into his audience. MTV was aimed at twelve to twenty-four-year olds who were only interested in the trends of the moment. Since Gen Xers were VH1's target audience, Graden decided to target their tastes by leveraging the nostalgia factor. By the mid-2000s Gen Xers were experiencing a definite love affair with all things pop culture. "We want to trigger the emotion from a past that we share together," Graden explained to Megan Larson. "The appetite for recycled pop culture seems endless. It's comfort food." VH1 began serving up large portions of pop comfort food through such series as *I Love the '80s,* which was followed by *I Love the '70s*. Both feature highlights of movies, music, news, and fads specific to the featured decade, interspersed with commentary provided by celebrities and entertainment critics. Viewers responded and began coming back in droves. By 2004 VH1 was in full recovery and the network had nearly tripled its original programming.

The Graden factor

People in the entertainment industry expect even greater things from Graden in the future. He is a man who relentlessly pursues popular culture, and he is always on the lookout for the next big trend. "I am a voracious consumer of culture," he admitted to Alex Williams of *New York Metro,* "There will be a stack of ten new CDs on my table, and then I have to TiVo everything, and I read at least thirty magazines cover to cover every month. I just can't stop." He is also known as a man who is passionate about his job. His colleagues comment about his boyish enthusiasm, which sparks a similar zeal in others. According to Judy McGrath, president of MTV Networks Music Group, "Brian enjoys the sport of TV."

And there is no end to what the former boy wonder has in the network pipelines. On VH1, Graden continues to mine the penchant for the past with series such as *Super Secret TV Formulas*. At the same time, he tries to bridge the generational gap (he is in his forties now, after all) through shows like *In Tune,* which pairs contemporary artists with musicians who inspired them. For example, in 2004, John Mayer (1977–) took the stage with his idol, singer-songwriter Paul Simon (1941–). Although Graden is a whiz at predicting the future of television, he is not quite as certain about his next career move. When asked about his plans by Jeffrey Epstein of *The Advocate,* he simply shrugged and replied, "I have absolutely no idea. I just want to keep being true to the moment."

For More Information

Periodicals

Epstein, Jeffrey. "He Got His MTV." *The Advocate* (May 23, 2000): p. 76.

Nix, Jenny. "MTV's Graden on an Upward Curve." *Variety* (December 22, 1997): p. 28.

Poniewozik, James. "VH1: Gen X Nostalgia Central." *Time* (February 2, 2004).

Romano, Allison. "His Finger Is on the Pulse of Pop Culture." *Broadcasting & Cable* (September 8, 2003): p. 40.

Web Sites

Larson, Megan. "Behind the Makeover." *MediaWeek.com* (March 24, 2003) http://www.mediaweek.com/mediaweek/icopyright_display.jsp?vnu_content_id=1847775 (accessed August 1, 2004).

MTV Web site. http://www.mtv.com (accessed August 1, 2004).

Valania, Jonathan. "Last Night a VJ Saved My Life." *Philadelphia Weekly Online.* (April 24, 2002) http://www.philadelphiaweekly.com/archives/article.asp?ArtID=2154 (accessed on June 11, 2004).

VH1 Web site. http://www.vh1.com (accessed August 1, 2004).

Williams, Alex. "MTV's Real World." *New York Metro.com* (December 2, 2002) http://newyorkmetro.com/nymetro/arts/tv/n_8081/index.html (accessed August 1, 2004).

Brian Greene

February 9, 1963 • *New York, New York*

Physicist, author

u·x·l newsmakers • *volume 2*

With his hip New York wardrobe, salt-and-pepper hair, and quick grin, Brian Greene looks more like a forty-something Justin Timberlake than the scientist that he is. In fact, Greene is considered one of the top physicists in the United States and a leading expert in the field of superstring theory, which asserts that all matter is made up of tiny vibrating loops of energy. He is also perhaps one of the most famous scientists in the world, thanks to his 1999 best-selling book, *The Elegant Universe,* a guide to string theory for average readers. In 2004 Greene released *The Fabric of the Cosmos,* a book that explores space and time, and which promised to be equally successful. Because of his ability to explain in simple terms what some call "headache-inducing" concepts, Greene has been credited not only with introducing science to the masses, but encouraging them to care about it.

Boy with a different perspective

Brian Greene was born on February 9, 1963, in New York City. Early on, it was apparent that Greene was different. He was obviously gifted in math; at one point he was known to tape together squares of construction paper in order to multiply numbers with thirty digits. Greene also credits his father, Alan, a former vaudeville performer, with teaching him how to look at the world in different ways. He explained the game he and his father used to play to Bradley Jay of *The Atlantic*. While walking the streets of Manhattan, Greene and his dad would take turns describing what they saw from different perspectives. For example, if Brian saw a penny fall out of someone's pocket, he might

"The universe is rich and exciting, and there's stuff that can knock you over every day if you're privy to it."

pretend to be an ant on the coin talking about spiraling down to the ground on a copper disk.

By the time he was in grade school, Greene was so precocious in math that his frustrated sixth-grade teacher suggested he look for a tutor at nearby Columbia University. With a note from his teacher in hand, Greene and his sister went from office to office on the campus, and finally located a graduate student willing to work with the budding mathematician. The student, Neil Bellinson, studied with him every week until Greene graduated from Stuyvesant High School in 1980. After graduation Greene attended Harvard University in Cambridge, Massachusetts, where he majored in physics, the science of the interaction between matter and energy. In addition to his studies, he also pursued other interests that began in high school. For example, Greene ran cross-country and acted in musicals.

Greene graduated from Harvard in 1984, and as a Rhodes Scholar he traveled to England to study at Oxford University. Each year Rhodes Scholarships are given to the most outstanding scholars

Very Greene Analogies

In order to explain very complicated concepts Brian Greene often turns to everyday examples. For instance, one of the ideas central to string theory is that there are many more dimensions than the ones we are aware of. The problem is that they are so small they are difficult to detect. Greene suggests that a dimension may be invisible because of our perspective. Imagine, he says, that far off in the distance an ant is walking on a garden hose. From our vantage point, the garden hose looks simply like a one-dimensional line. If we walk closer, the ant and the garden hose, another dimension if you will, come into view.

Another example is Greene's explanation of the uncertainty principle, which was proposed by one of the greatest physicists of the twentieth century, Werner Heisenberg (1901–1976). According to Heisenberg, who spent his life studying the movement and properties of atoms, it is impossible to pinpoint the precise position and momentum of a particle at the same time. In his "Strings and Strings" lecture, as quoted in *Columbia College Today,* Greene likens the principle to ordering dinner from a Chinese menu: "There's list A and list B. You can have Chow Mein, you can have Mu Shu, but under no circumstances, according to Heisenberg, can you have both."

in the world; the scholarships allow them to study at the prestigious Oxford University. In his spare time, Greene acted with an improvisational theater group. This knack for acting would one day serve him well, as he became known for his easy and relaxed public speaking style. Greene's focus at Oxford, however, was physics.

It was at Oxford that Greene first became intrigued by string theory. As he was walking to class one day he spied a poster advertising a lecture about a newfound "theory of everything." "I found it very exciting," Greene told Shira Boss of *Columbia College Today.* "They were saying there was a brand new way to solve the riddle of gravity and quantum mechanics." After attending the lecture, he and his friends formed a study group and absorbed any and all information on the subject they could find.

String theory is the key

After earning his PhD in physics in 1987, Greene returned to Harvard. In 1990 he took a teaching job at Cornell University in Ithaca, New York, where he became a full professor in 1995. The next year Columbia University recruited him to teach physics and math. Greene remains a professor there to this day, and is codirector of the school's Institute for Strings, Cosmology, and Astroparticle Physics. He also teaches at Cornell and Duke University in Durham, North Carolina, via teleconferencing. Greene became known as a dynamic lecturer and his classes, though covering difficult subjects, were in high demand. As one student remarked to Boss, "He breaks things down in the most basic language. It makes it engaging and enjoyable, which is why we've been hanging on for so long, even though the concepts are fuzzy."

Fuzzy is probably the right word to describe string theory, which is the focus of Greene's research. According to Greene, in an interview with Jay, "the basic idea of string theory is pretty straightforward. It tries to answer a question that has been asked for two-and-a-half thousand years, which is, What are the smallest ingredients making up everything in the world around us?" The difficult part is that string theorists claim the building blocks of the universe are filaments, or strings, that vibrate at various frequencies. These strings are so small that they cannot be observed; they cannot even be proven through experiments. Instead, Greene and his colleagues rely on mathematics to infer their existence.

Some wonder why it is important to worry about something so small that it cannot be seen. According to Greene and other physicists, string theory holds the key to unlocking everything, including how the universe was created and how it works. The mathematics of string theory also speculates about even more fantastic ideas, including the belief that there are eleven dimensions, seven more than we are currently aware of; and that several parallel universes exist alongside our own. Greene became well known in the scientific community for championing these theories. In 1992 he and two Duke University colleagues also made an amazing discovery. Using advanced mathematics they were able to prove that the fabric of space can tear and then repair itself in a new way. As Greene told Peter Tyson of *NOVA,* "For a brief moment, you feel like you have seen the universe in a way that nobody previously has."

Physics becomes fun

Greene, along with his discoveries, would probably have remained known to only a handful of academics, except that in the late 1990s he was approached to write a book about string theory. At first he was reluctant, worrying that he might not be able to successfully produce something that could be understood by the general public. The biggest hurdle was that string theory is proven through mathematical symbols, which cannot easily be translated into everyday language. But Greene also saw a need. As he remarked to Shira Boss, "People can be turned off from science, because the technical side can be forbidding, but the ideas are as dramatic as any novel." In 1999 Greene succeeded in his efforts, and *The Elegant Universe: Superstrings, Hidden Dimensions, and the Quest for the Ultimate Theory* was published.

The book took off immediately, breaking sales records, and zooming up nearly every U.S. best-seller list. What followed was a media blitz. Greene was scheduled for a multitude of book signings, and he appeared on countless radio and television programs from National Public Radio's *Science Friday* to the *Late Show with David Letterman*. Suddenly Greene was a celebrity physicist. He was even stopped on the street by fans and well-wishers. Why would a book about string theory be so popular? According to *Publishers Weekly,* "the strength of the book resided in Greene's unparalleled ability to translate higher mathematics and its findings into everyday language and images, through adept use of metaphor and analogy, and crisp, witty prose." It probably also did not hurt that the thirty-six-year-old Greene was just as witty when he appeared in person.

Greene was happy about the brisk book sales, but he was equally happy that he was generating a buzz about string theory, and science in general. Perhaps the greatest testament of his success came in the letters and e-mails that he received from people of all ages. For example, Shira Boss quoted one man who described himself as a "playwright and independent filmmaker who got a D in high school physics." He wrote to Greene: "You have given science back to me, and for that, I owe you an immeasurable gratitude."

Understanding the cosmos

Four years later, in 2003, Greene helped *NOVA* translate *The Elegant Universe* into a three-hour documentary. Creating a movie was an incredibly ambitious undertaking since Greene discusses concepts that cannot be seen, let alone filmed. The producers used state-of-the-art computer animation, special effects, and trick photography to help viewers delve into Greene's universe. They also relied on Greene's wide-ranging talents as an enthusiastic storyteller and gifted performer. The physicist-turned-filmmaker, however, wanted to make sure that the documentary was both entertaining and accurate. "For me," he explained to *NOVA's* Peter Tyson, "it was constantly keeping a watch out to make sure that the science ultimately was dictating what we could and couldn't do."

In 2004 Greene again put ambition to the test when he released his second book, *The Fabric of the Cosmos: Space, Time, and the Texture of Reality.* While *The Elegant Universe* focused on superstring theory, *Fabric,* as Greene told Tyson, is a "discussion of our ever-changing grasp of what these seemingly simple notions of space and time actually are." In what *Library Journal* called "simple but elegant language," Greene attempts to explain even more complex concepts for the general reader. He uses his usual clever analogies, including frogs in bowls, pennies on balloons, and ping-pong balls in molasses, to help us understand how time travel might be possible or how time does not flow the way we think it does. Greene also peppers the text with pop-culture allusions, including references to such popular TV shows as *The Simpsons.*

Not all reviews were positive, however. *The Economist* maintained that Greene fell short of his intentions and that his second book comprised a "meandering path through the maze of modern physics … which is highly confusing to the novice." Regardless, the public welcomed the latest offering from the Columbia physicist.

The elegant Professor Greene

In between dates on his multi-city publicity tour, Greene continued to teach his classes, which had become packed with students and non-students clamoring to attend. He was also busy giving public lectures in an attempt to reach an even wider audience. Working with the Emerson String Quartet, he developed a type of performance art that blended physics and music. Called "Strings and Strings," the charismatic Greene lectured to audience members, essentially giving them a crash course in physics, all set against a symphonic backdrop. The event drew sell-out crowds to the Guggenheim Museum in New York City, and there were plans to develop a full-length program to be presented at New York's Lincoln Center in 2005.

Greene also planned to begin work on a series of books aimed at young children that would help prepare them to digest more difficult physics books as they get older. In addition, he envisioned a companion film that would be entertaining and story-based. According to Jeff Zaleski of *Publishers Weekly,* Greene will no doubt, make "science a blast to watch." But for Greene there is a more important mission. He truly believes that understanding physics, and understanding the way the universe works, is essential for each and every person. As he told Zaleski, "I've seen that, as people become aware of space and time, of the strange events of quantum mechanics, they are enriched because they see the world in a different way." He likens it to baseball or football; if you know the rules you enjoy watching the game so much more.

Greene maintains a balance between his work and his personal life, although he admits that his job is not just nine-to-five. He continues to take acting lessons, which as he explained to Shira Boss, provides a release, "a way to enter a new world. The things you think about [when acting] are totally different from what you think of in a normal research day." Greene also maintains a healthy respect for the world around him. He lives in Andes, New York, on an old farm that he hopes one day to transform into an animal shelter. He also follows a vegan diet, which means he eats no animals or animal byproducts, such as milk or cheese.

When it comes to his research, as important as he considers it to be, Greene is sometimes frustrated by it. He has spent almost twenty years of his life working on a theory that may or may not be right. "It's a very precarious way to live and to work," he admitted to Tyson. On the other hand, Greene believes that his research has paved the way for other important developments. In the same interview, he told Tyson, "To me if the theory turns out to be right, that will be tremendously thick and tasty icing on the cake."

For More Information

Books

Greene, Brian. *The Elegant Universe: Superstrings, Hidden Dimensions, and the Quest for the Ultimate Theory.* New York: W. W. Norton, 1999.

Greene, Brian. *The Fabric of the Cosmos: Space, Time, and the Texture of Reality.* New York: Alfred A. Knopf, 2004.

Periodicals

"All Strung Out: Popular Physics." Review of *The Fabric of the Cosmos: Space, Time, and the Texture of Reality. The Economist* (April 17, 2004): p. 83.

Buczynski, James A. Review of *The Fabric of the Cosmos. Library Journal* (March 15, 2004): p. 103.

Kirschling, Gregory. "Master of the Universe." *Entertainment Weekly* (February 27, 2004): p. 101.

Review of *The Fabric of the Cosmos. Publishers Weekly* (February 9, 2004): p. 74.

Zaleski, Jeff. "Writing Science: Inside the Elegant Universe of Brian Greene." *Publishers Weekly* (February 9, 2004): pp. 50–54.

Web Sites

Boss, Shira. "World on a String." *Columbia College Today* (September 1999) http://www.college.columbia.edu/cct/sep99/12a.html (accessed August 1, 2004).

The Elegant Universe Web site. http://www.pbs.org/wgbh/nova/elegant (accessed August 1, 2004).

Jay, Bradley. "The Universe Made Simple." *Atlantic Unbound* (May 20, 2004). http://www.theatlantic.com/unbound/interviews/int2004-05-20.htm (accessed August 1, 2004).

Tyson, Peter and Brian Greene. "Elegant Universe: Conversation with Brian Greene." *Nova Online* (July 2003). http://www.pbs.org/wgbh/nova/elegant/greene.html (accessed August 1, 2004).

Helen Greiner

AP/Wide World Photos. Reproduced by permission.

1967 • *London, England*

Roboticist, president and cofounder of iRobot Corporation

For roboticist Helen Greiner the future is not found in the pages of a science fiction novel; the future is here and now. As president and cofounder of the iRobot Corporation, she is responsible for helping to advance the accessibility of robots, which are mechanical devices that perform functions automatically or by remote control. Most of iRobot's inventions have been designed for use in the military or in industry, but with technology costs decreasing, the company's consumer robot market is starting to take off. Greiner predicts that within a few years almost every home in the United States will have a robot to perform such tasks as housecleaning and babysitting. Her company's vision, as she told Elizabeth Durant of *Technology Review,* is to "get robots into everyone's hands."

A fan of R2D2

Helen Greiner was born in London, England, in 1967. Her father was a refugee from Hungary who met his future wife at the University of London. When she was five years old, the family moved to the United States where they settled in Southampton, New York, a suburb of New York City. Even when she was young, Greiner was a whiz at science. Her older brother had all sorts of neat radio-controlled cars and electronics sets and Greiner was so jealous that, as she admitted to *Dataquest,* she "sometimes took them." When her family bought one of the earliest personal computers (PCs), a TRS-80 purchased from Radio Shack, Greiner claimed it for her own. She spent a good deal of time tinkering with it and fine-tuning it, and soon she was using it to control the movements of some of her brother's confiscated toys.

> **"If we don't take robots to the next level, we'll have a lot of explaining to do to our grandchildren."**

In 1977, when she was only ten years old, Greiner went to see a movie that would point to her future life's work. That movie was *Star Wars.* While most girls developed crushes on Luke Skywalker or Han Solo, Greiner was captivated by the three-foot-tall spunky android, R2D2. "He was not just a machine," she told *Dataquest.* "He had moods, emotions, and dare I say, his own agenda. This was exciting to me—he was a creature, an artificial creature." When the ten-year-old found out that R2D2 was actually controlled by a man inside a plastic-cased costume she was crushed. From that day, Greiner vowed to create her own R2D2, a real one based on state-of-the-art technology.

That vow prompted Greiner to attend Massachusetts Institute of Technology (MIT), one of the finest colleges for science and technology in the world. While at MIT she dove into the study of robotics and artificial intelligence (AI). AI is the computer technology that allows robots to react to situations and gives them some ability to reason. Greiner worked in MIT's Artificial Intelligence Laboratory, which was (and still is) headed by Rodney Brooks (1954–), the man who would one day be Greiner's partner at iRobot. Greiner also met Colin Angle at MIT; Angle would become the third partner in the iRobot venture. The two actually became acquainted on Greiner's first day on

Robots Meet the Past: iRobot in Egypt

The iRobot Corporation designs and builds robots that do all kinds of extraordinary things, from climbing walls to squeezing through narrow pipes. In the summer of 2002, however, one of the company's robots visited the past. Earlier in the year iRobot was approached by the science and exploration magazine *National Geographic* and Egypt's Supreme Council of Antiquities to build a robot that would explore two of the shafts, or tunnels, in the Great Pyramid of Giza. The pyramid, located near Cairo, Egypt, was built around 2650 B.C.E by the Egyptian pharaoh Khufu (Cheops) to serve as a tomb when he died.

The two shafts in question, a northern one and a southern one, both lead to the Queen's chamber. In the early 1990s, a German archaeologist had attempted to explore the southern shaft using a robot, but was thwarted in his efforts because the shaft was blocked as it neared the chamber. Shortly after being contacted, iRoboters went to work. First, they built a test shaft that represented the angle, height, and width of the pyramid's shaft. Then they quickly designed and built the tiny Pyramid Rover, which is only approximately 5 inches wide and 11 inches long. It can expand and contract in height from 4 to 11 inches, which made navigating through the shaft easy since it could grip the top and bottom for better stability.

The Rover was tied to a controller outside the pyramid and was equipped with lights, video equipment, and tools specific to archaeology. When it made its journey through the southern shaft it performed remarkably. Upon reaching the blocking stone, it used a gauge to figure out the thickness of the rock; the Rover then drilled a small hole through the block and inserted a tiny camera using its extending arm. Since the expedition was televised on the Fox Network, millions of people around the world were given the first glimpse into the Queen's chamber, which had been sealed for 4,500 years.

campus. They became fast friends because they were both devoted to the science of robots; they were also big snowboarding fans.

iRobot comes to life

Before Greiner graduated in 1989 with a bachelor's degree in mechanical engineering she spent some time in Pasadena, California, interning at NASA's Jet Propulsion Laboratory. Her job was to help design robots that would do repairs in space. Her interest was sparked enough that she developed designs for a space robot that could grasp objects more easily. The designs became part of her master's thesis. In 1990, after earning an advanced degree in computer science, Greiner headed back to California to work at California Cybernetics, a company that made robots which helped in the manufacture of cars. Less than a year later she returned to the East Coast to form her own robot company with Brooks and Angle.

The three roboticists had a very simple plan: to build affordable robots that could be used in everyday life. A simple plan, but ambitious since the robotics field was in its early infancy. When Greiner and her colleagues first started out, she likened it to the early days of computers in the 1970s. The few robots that existed were very expensive, costing tens of thousands of dollars, and they were used mostly in manufacturing, especially in the auto industry to complete such tasks as spray-painting or welding. Most of the experimentation was being done in university research labs, and that is where it usually stopped; there was very little practical application. As Greiner told *Dataquest:* "I saw the work going on in research labs and universities. It was really great stuff, but it all seemed to die when the funding ran out, or when the student left. I found this really appalling." She went on to explain, "Commercial successes will drive the innovation."

Calling their company IS Robotics, the MIT partners set up shop in Angle's apartment. Greiner was named president, Angle became the chief executive officer, and Brooks took on the role of chief technology officer. They started out building robots for university researchers at a cost of $3,000 each. Since they only sold about sixty per year, and the cost of parts was steep, the company barely broke even. The partners worked eighteen-hour days, writing their own computer codes and soldering parts, parts that were frequently built in MIT's machine shop. Eventually they were able to hire a handful of other engineers, but they also recruited interns from MIT who were paid minimum wage. They were so dedicated to their vision that they put up all the manufacturing costs themselves, maxing out their credit cards and racking up over $100,000 in bank loans.

Military-minded: Ariel and PackBot

The company's first big government contract came in 1993 when it was hired by the U.S. Department of Defense and the Office of Naval Research to design an underwater minesweeper. As they do with many of their creations, company engineers modeled the robot, called the Ariel Underwater, after a living creature. In this case, the model was the ghost crab, a burrowing crustacean that lives on Atlantic and Caribbean beaches. Like the ghost crab, Ariel has six legs and can sway with the tides while still maintaining a grip on the ocean floor. It is programmed

I, Robot: The Movie

The iRobot Corporation was named after a series of short stories written by Isaac Asimov (1920–1992), a popular American science fiction writer who wrote countless books and who many consider to be one of the greatest writers in the genre. Asimov is credited with actually coining the term *robotics*. He also developed what he called the "Three Laws of Robotics*:*

1. A robot may not harm or injure a human being.

2. A robot must obey the orders that a human being gives to it, unless it would result in injury.

3. A robot must protect its own existence as long as it does not interfere with laws number one or two.

In July of 2004 a movie based on Asimov's stories was released by 20th Century Fox, called *I, Robot.* The film starred Will Smith (1968–) as a detective of the future investigating the death of a scientist at a company called US Robotics. Despite the Laws of Robotics, his primary suspect in the killing is a robot. The robots featured in the movie are called NS-5 models, known as the "world's first fully automated domestic assistant." In conjunction with the movie's release, 20th Century Fox launched an interactive Web site (www.irobotnow.com), which gave viewers a glimpse into the making of the movie bot; it also allowed users to virtually build their own NS-5.

to detect mines, explosives set in the ground or under the water; it can also place explosives and scurry away before they blow up.

Boosted by their success, the partners moved into headquarters based in Somerville, Massachusetts. They also hired more engineers and changed the company name to iRobot. According to Greiner the name comes from a book of short stories written in 1950 by noted science fiction author Isaac Asimov (1920–1992). In addition, the company began to take on some nonmilitary work. For example, they contracted with the oil-service company Baker Hughes to design a robot that could travel miles underground to make repairs in oil-well bores. The bulk of iRobot's business, however, remained focused on creating products for the military.

Greiner and company turned a corner in 1995 when the Defense Department commissioned them to make what would become one of their premier products: a small tank-like robot, known as the PackBot, designed to scope out areas too dangerous for soldiers. At forty pounds it is portable; it is also able to climb stairs, travel over even the toughest terrain, and can right itself, using flippers, if knocked over.

After the World Trade Center in New York City was destroyed in 2001, four PackBots were sent into nearby buildings to make sure the structures were sound. In 2002 the robots were first used in combat when they were sent to Afghanistan. Their mission was to search caves for enemy soldiers and to sniff out booby traps. At first U.S. soldiers were skeptical. As Greiner told Elizabeth Durant of *Technology Review,* "The guys were like, 'Robots? We don't need robots. We were trained how to clear caves.' But when you get to the cave's mouth, and it's dark inside … they started calling for the robots."

Based on feedback from the field, the company was able to tweak the PackBot's design. In 2003 PackBots were sent to Iraq to search buildings, vehicles, and airfields for booby traps and mines. The robots are equipped with a camera that can transmit images back to the base. Some of the PackBots are even capable of detecting harmful gases. By 2004 estimates, approximately fifty PackBots were being used in Iraq and Afghanistan and only one of them had been lost in action.

Oh, baby! Company breaks into consumer market

Regardless of her success, Greiner's main goal was still to break into the consumer market with something affordable and practical. The company's first foray into the consumer market was definitely more affordable than the PackBot, which had a price tag of $45,000, but it was more fun than truly practical. In the late 1990s, iRobot partnered with the Hasbro toy company to develop a robotic doll. Engineers worked on the design for almost two years, equipping the doll's skin with electronic sensors so that it giggled when its feet were tickled and smiled when it was held. The doll was also programmed to "learn" to speak.

Called My Real Baby, the toy hit store shelves in 2000. Considering the doll was quite expensive to produce, at $95.95 it was fairly reasonably priced. Not reasonable enough for customers, however, since Hasbro sold only 100,000 units. Greiner still considered the product to be a company milestone since it paved the way for advancements in artificial intelligence. Rodney Brooks, who spoke with Joseph Pereira, explained that, "for the first time our robots had

to interact with countless numbers of people in ordinary homes, not graduate students [in labs]."

In 2002 iRobot introduced the product that finally put it firmly on the consumer map, a disc-shaped robotic vacuum cleaner called the Roomba. Engineers had been working on the design for twelve years. They also put in countless hours studying the science of floor-cleaning; iRoboters even spent one night at a Target department store to watch industrial cleaners at work. The result was a 5-pound, 13-inch-wide appliance that looks very much like a horseshoe crab. It runs on rechargeable batteries and propels around a room in wide circles, bouncing lightly off any obstacle it encounters. When it is finished, it stops, beeps, and turns itself off.

According to the company, Roomba has enjoyed brisk sales. It also received wide publicity on television, radio, and in countless magazines. Oprah Winfrey (1954–) named it "one of her favorite things," and the Roomba was awarded the seal of approval from *Good Housekeeping,* a magazine that has long served consumers. In addition, iRobot and Roomba received hearty approval within the robotics industry. As Craig Jennings, president of the Robotic Industries Association, told Elizabeth Durant, "Nobody else has a product that has had the success of Roomba. I think [iRobot] hit a home run."

Greiner predictions

By 2004 the tiny company that was started in a scientist's apartment employed over 120 people, and was based in Burlington, Massachusetts, with branch offices in Milford, New Hampshire, and San Luis Obispo, California. It had contracts in multiple markets, including academic, industrial, military, and consumer, which made it the largest, privately owned robotics company in the world. The corporation's mission, however, remained roughly the same. As stated on the iRobot Web site, the partners pledge "to build really cool stuff; to make money; to have fun; and to change the world."

Because of the company's growth and success, its founders, especially Greiner, began to receive quite a bit of recognition. In 2002 Greiner was named an Innovator for the Next Century by MIT's *Technology Review*; in 2003, she made *Fortune* magazine's list of the Top 10 Innovators Under 40 in the United States. According to Greiner, however, iRobot was just beginning to take off. "There's so much room for innovation and new ideas," she commented to Kristin Weir of *Current Science.*

Greiner's predictions for the future of robotics are great. She told Deepa Kandasamy of *Dataquest* that according to U.S. military officials within fifteen years, "one-third of all military vehicles will be unmanned." She also believes that given the advancements in AI technology and the drop in costs for robot components, such as computer chips, consumer products will become even more affordable. "Within five years robots will be cleaning floors and acting as remote eyes and ears," Greiner enthused to Kandasamy, "Within fifteen years, they will act as true personal assistants and friends." When asked about her personal vision, Greiner, whose corporate office is strewn with toy robots, replied that she sees "our robots taking on all dangerous jobs. A robot in every office building. A robot in every home that has a computer. We will change the world with this technology."

For More Information

Periodicals

Durant, Elizabeth. "Robot-Triumvirate: A Robotic Vacuum Cleaner Is Putting iRobot and Its Three Founders on the Map." *Technology Review* (October 2003).

Pope, Justin. "Looking to Iraq, Military Robots Focus on Lessons of Afghanistan." *Detroit News* (January 12, 2003).

Weir, Kirsten. "Robot Master." *Current Science* (February 28, 2003): p. 8.

Web Sites

"Ancient Egyptian Chambers Explored." *National Geographic Channel Web site* (April 4, 2003). http://news.nationalgeographic.com/news/ 2002/09/0910_020913_egypt_1.html (accessed August 1, 2004).

Goldman, Leah. "Machine Dreams." *Forbes.com* (May 27, 2002). http:// www.forbes.com/global/2002/0527/043.html (accessed August 1, 2004).

Grossman, Lev. "Maid to Order." *Time.com* (September 14, 2002). http:// www.time.com/time/roomba (accessed August 1, 2004).

iRobot Corporation Web site. http://www.irobot.com/home.cfm (accessed August 1, 2004).

I, Robot Now Web site. http://www.irobotnow.com/index.php (accessed August 1 2004).

Kandasamy, Deepa. "Queen of Robotics." *Dataquest Web site*. (March 17, 2004) http://www.dqindia.com/content/industrymarket/datatalk/2004/ 104031701.asp (accessed August 1, 2004).

Pereira, Joseph. "Natural Intelligence: Helen Greiner Thinks Robots Are Ready to Become Part of the Household." *Wall Street Journal: Classroom Edition Online*. (October 2002) http://www.wsjclassroomedition. com/archive/02oct/COVR_ROBOT.htm (accessed August 1, 2004).

NORTHEASTERN
MIDDLE SCHOOL LIBRARY

Josh Groban

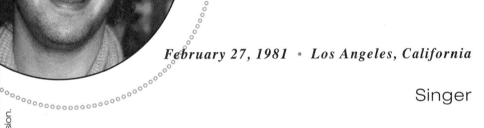

AP/Wide World Photos. Reproduced by permission.

February 27, 1981 • Los Angeles, California

Singer

Josh Groban is not a typical twenty-something pop singer, and record store owners have had a tough time deciding just what bin to put his CDs in. Many of his songs are contemporary romantic ballads, but Groban, who is classically trained, also performs opera and sings classical songs in Italian, Spanish, and French. Regardless of the fact that he defies classification, Groban's fans number in the millions, and they have no problem locating or buying his music. Since bursting on the scene with his debut album in 2002, the gangly Groban has become a music phenomenon. He was the best-selling new male artist of 2002, and since then he has toured the world, performing to record-breaking crowds of all ages.

A unique voice

Joshua Winslow Groban was born February 27, 1981, in Los Angeles, California. According to Groban, both of his parents were quite artistic and instilled in their children a love of theater and music. His mother, Melinda, was an artist and interior designer. His father, Jack, a businessman who owned his own executive recruiting company, was an accomplished pianist who could play piano by ear. Groban inherited his piano-playing skills from his father. He also credits both his parents for introducing him to a wide variety of musical styles.

Groban was drawn to musical theater and opera, counting Mandy Patinkin (1952–) and Luciano Pavarotti (1935–) as two of his idols. At the same time, he listened to pop musicians. In *Interview,* Groban explained to Renee Fleming that he was especially interested in artists "who decided not to settle into one particular musical style—people like Paul Simon, who took folk music and put African

> **"I'm not performing for the classical crowd or the Britney crowd. I'm performing for people who like all different kinds of music."**

music on top of it." He was referring to American singer-songwriter Paul Simon (1941–) and his award-winning *Graceland* album, which was the first CD Groban ever received as a gift.

Although he was inspired by music from an early age, Groban was not an early singer. He eventually took a vocal class in junior high school, but as he admitted on his Web site, he really joined because all the other kids were joining. A turning point came in the seventh grade when his teacher auditioned students to sing in the school's variety show. Groban wowed the teacher with his voice and was tapped to perform a solo. The number was a song written in the 1920s by the famous American composers George (1898–1937) and Ira Gershwin (1896–1983). While it showcased Groban's rich voice, it did not make him particularly popular with kids his own age. "When you're in the seventh grade and everybody's listening to rap, it's not the coolest thing to discover you have a voice like mine," he told Fleming.

After the performance, however, Groban had a revelation. As he explained to Fleming, "I realized that this was something I could do to stand out and express myself in a way that I didn't normally know how to do. And that became something very powerful." As Groban grew older and his voice matured, it became apparent that he had real talent. He was accepted into the Los Angeles County High School for the Arts, where he studied musical theater and acted in many school plays, in the hope that one day he would sing and act professionally. The chance came sooner than he expected.

Opera boy in the making

When he was seventeen years old, Groban's voice teacher, Seth Riggs, was contacted by Grammy Award-winning producer and composer David Foster (c. 1950–), who was looking for someone to sing at some upcoming celebrity events. Riggs sent Foster tapes from several of his students, but it was Groban's recording that caught Foster's attention. "It floored me," the producer told *People* in 2002. Foster immediately booked him to perform at the 1999 inauguration of California Governor Gray Davis (1942–), which took place in Sacramento, California. A very nervous Groban found himself singing in front of a crowd of twenty thousand.

A few weeks later, Celine Dion (c. 1968–) was slated to sing a duet with Italian opera star Andrea Bocelli (1958–) on the Grammy Awards program. Bocelli, however, was unable to rehearse, and Foster asked Groban to fill in. At first Groban said no, since he was given only a few hours' notice. "I didn't want to go in there unprepared," he told Bob Brown of *ABC News*. He relented, however, realizing that this was a once-in-a-lifetime opportunity. When he took the stage with Dion, he was enthusiastically praised as the young man with the impressively grown-up voice. Comedian Rosie O'Donnell (1962–), who was hosting the awards program, took a quick liking to Groban and invited him to appear on her talk show, dubbing him Opera Boy.

Foster continued his partnership with Groban, and invited him to perform at a number of high-profile events. At one of these events, Groban drew the interest of television writer and producer David E. Kelley (1956–). At the time, Kelley was working on the hit TV series *Ally McBeal* and thought that Groban would be perfect for an upcoming episode. In the show's 2001 season finale, Groban appeared as Malcolm Wyatt, a nerdy high school senior who sues a fellow classmate for breaking their prom date. Of course, Kelley made sure that Groban's singing was a key part of the script. After the episode aired, thousands of viewers called and wrote in to the Fox network inquiring about the talented young newcomer.

Special marketing for a special singer

Meanwhile, Groban had graduated from high school and was planning to attend Carnegie Mellon University in Pittsburgh, Pennsylvania, to continue studying musical theater. Foster, however, approached him with the news that executives at 143 Records, a joint venture between Foster and Warner Brothers, were interested in signing a record deal. Groban thought long and hard, but ultimately decided to put college on the back burner and take the plunge into the music business.

Initially, record company executives were not sure how to approach Groban's first album. With his boyish good looks, they first thought that Groban should focus on pop songs. But his classical training prompted them to consider an album including Italian opera. In the end, Foster stepped in and worked to produce Groban's 2001 self-titled debut album, which included a blend of contemporary rock and pop tunes along with classical music in English, Spanish, and Italian. Such a combination was difficult to market in the fast-paced world of MTV, so the record company took a variety of approaches to promote their new artist.

Groban was invited back to appear on a holiday episode of *Ally McBeal* in late 2001. He also appeared on numerous talk shows, from *Oprah* to the *Tonight Show with Jay Leno*. Groban was even featured on the prime-time news program *20/20*. Following the media blitz, album sales soared and Josh Groban Web sites popped up all over the Internet. But the media blitz was just getting started. Groban went on to make countless public appearances, with one major highlight coming in early 2002. When he took the stage to sing with Welsh soprano Charlotte Church (1986–) at the closing ceremony of the Winter Olympics in Salt Lake City, Utah, Groban was heard by an estimated 1.6 billion people around the world.

In late 2002 Groban was given a major opportunity when he taped a live concert that was aired on PBS in December. The twenty-year-old took the stage with a variety of music heavyweights, including Andrea Corr (1974–), lead singer of the Irish traditional/pop group The Corrs, and the legendary American composer John Williams (1932–). At the same time, Groban released his second album, *Josh Groban in Concert,* a DVD-CD combination based on the PBS special. It debuted at number thirty-five on the *Billboard* Top 200 chart and quickly reached number one on the music video charts.

Closer to Groban

Thanks to an unprecedented amount of media coverage, Groban's fan base grew by leaps and bounds. He was especially popular on the Internet, where his CD enjoyed increasing sales. One record executive, as quoted on *ABC News,* called him "the first Internet star." An on-line community of fans who called themselves Grobanites helped to boost sales. Another site called Friends of Josh Groban became a one-stop shopping network where fans could order concert tickets, albums, and get up-to-the-minute news about their favorite singer.

Fans did not have to wait too long to hear more of Groban, since he was back in the studio in 2003 to put together his third album. For seven months he worked with producers to choose, arrange, and record songs. Groban also spent time writing songs, three of which appeared on the final cut. As he explained on his Web site, "This time I've tried to open the door as wide as possible. These songs are a giant step closer to who I really am and what my music is all about." As a result, the album was titled *Closer.* As exhilarating as the experience was, however, Groban admitted that it was also daunting. In the same Web site article he confided, "I felt tremendous pressure to repeat the success of the first album.... The challenge became not so much reaching the bar I had already set, but setting it higher."

When *Closer* was released in late 2003, it received mixed reviews. While most critics praised Groban's powerhouse voice, they also believed that his delivery was somewhat immature and lackluster. Reviewers were especially critical of Groban's pop songs. Chuck Arnold of *People* called them "over-the-top ballads," and Scott Paulin of *Entertainment Weekly* dismissed them as "depressingly predictable." Arnold went on to suggest that Groban, with his classically trained voice, should stick to singing in Italian, Spanish, and French.

"As it is," Arnold wrote, "this is a disc only Groban-ites will love." And Grobanites did love it. The first week it was released, *Closer* rocketed to number four on the *Billboard* chart, and by mid-2004 it had sold more than four million copies.

In January of 2004 Groban embarked on his first world concert tour, with stops slated in the United States, France, England, Norway, and Sweden. When tickets went on sale, they sold out almost immediately. Fans of all ages flocked to Groban's shows, which were decidedly more mellow than the usual rock concert. In an interview with Bob Meadows of *People,* Groban joked that "the security guards at my shows don't have anything to do." Fans may have been more well-behaved, but they were also incredibly devoted. One woman told Meadows that she had seen Groban in concert forty-four times. People in the music industry were amazed at the sellout crowds, but one *Billboard* insider, Geoff Mayfield, tried to explain the phenomenon in *People*: "I think it's a personal connection. [Groban] seems accessible as a human being, with that otherworldly voice."

Josh Groban performs at the 2004 Super Bowl. © Win McNamee/ Reuters/Corbis.

A little bit of everything

Since being discovered by Foster in 1999, Groban has been working almost nonstop, either traveling, performing, or in the recording studio. He does not complain, but does admit that life on the road is not that glamorous. Days are long and filled with voice lessons, sound checks, and rehearsals. To pass the time, he reads, watches movies, and plays video games. Groban is also an avid drummer. He learned to play when he was about sixteen years old, and as he explained to Fleming, "It's a great way to get all the stress out."

Few young people gain so much success at so early an age, but Groban seems to be handling it well. He commented that his biggest extravagance has been to buy a Porsche. He also views his career with a mature eye. While he is trained to sing opera, he does not see himself recording or performing any major arias for some time. "When I do them," he told Fleming, "I want to do them right." And Groban still has his sights set on Broadway. He came one step closer to his dream in September of 2003, when he appeared in a one-night-only benefit performance of the play *Chess* at the Amsterdam Theater in New York City. There appears to be much more ahead for the boy with the "bottomless lungs." When asked by Fleming where he sees himself in ten years, he replied, "I'd like to be able to say that I put my foot in a little of everything, but that I did it intelligently. And if I make mistakes, I want to know that I learned from them."

For More Information

Periodicals

Arnold, Chuck. Review of *Closer*. *People* (December 1, 2003): p. 46.

Fleming, Renee. "Josh Groban: So How Did Josh Groban Manage to Woo Millions of Hearts with Just His Set of Prodigious Pipes?" *Interview* (March 2004): pp. 140–145.

Meadows, Bob. "Josh Groban: Why are Grandmothers and Tweeners Screaming Their Heads Off at the Same Concert? To Catch America's Hottest Crooner." *People* (June 21, 2004): p. 117.

Paulin, Scott. Review of *Closer*. *Entertainment Weekly* (November 14, 2003): p. 122.

"A Stella is Born: Baby Baritone Josh Groban Adds Italian Dressing to the Music Charts with a New Classical-Pop Album." *People* (June 17, 2002): p. 116

Web Sites

Brown, Bob. "A Star in the Making: Who is Josh Groban?." *ABCNews. com: 20/20* http://www.abcnews.go.com/sections/2020/DailyNews/2020_joshgroban_020412.html (accessed on June 20, 2004).

Josh Groban Web site. http://www.joshgroban.com (accessed on June 18, 2004).

Tony Hawk

AP/Wide World Photos. Reproduced by permission.

May 12, 1968 • *San Diego, California*

Skateboarder, businessman

According to *Newsweek* magazine, Tony Hawk is the "most famous skateboarder, like, ever." A big claim, but with a lot to support it. In the 1980s and 1990s, Hawk almost single-handedly transformed skateboarding from a kids' parking-lot pastime into a respected sport. He won virtually every skateboarding competition he entered, and before he was twenty, he was considered to be the number one vertical skateboarder in the world.

Hawk was equally talented off the ramp. His business ventures and product endorsements have made him a very wealthy man, and have also kept him in the spotlight. As skateboarding icon Stacy Peralta told *Sports Illustrated*, "Tony is the first skateboarder who has given the world a face to put on the sport. He has become a part of American pop culture."

Skateboarding to the rescue

When Anthony Frank Hawk was born on May 12, 1968, his parents could not have realized that skateboarding was eventually going to become such an integral part of their lives. As Hawk readily admitted in his autobiography, he was a "hyperactive demon child" who regularly terrorized his babysitters, his teachers, and his parents. He was very bright, with an IQ of 144, but he was also frustrated and unfocused, and would frequently fly into rages. His father, Frank, a retired U.S. Navy officer and small appliance salesman, and his mother, Nancy, a homemaker and part-time business teacher, were equally frustrated about what to do with their youngest child. When Hawk

---

"I feel like if I'm not out there getting banged up, then I'm not getting better."

---

was eight, his older brother Steve bought him, on a whim, a blue fiberglass hand-me-down skateboard, and his father built a skating ramp in the backyard. They hoped that skateboarding might be the outlet that young Tony needed.

Hawk was instantly hooked, and soon the young boy with the behavior problems was practicing up to six hours a day, every day. He especially enjoyed the freedom that came with the sport. As he explained to Charlie Rose of *CBS News,* skateboarding was not like baseball or basketball, which required teamwork and regular practice schedules. "I liked that no one was telling me how to do it," he remarked. When Hawk outgrew his backyard ramp, he began practicing at skateparks near his home in San Diego, California. The scrawny kid with the wild blonde hair stood out among the other skaters. He was so skinny that he had to wear elbow pads on his knees, but the young skateboarder was already experimenting with daredevil moves.

Frank Hawk, realizing that the sport had virtually saved his son, became the ultimate skateboard supporter and Tony Hawk's number-one fan. He began by driving Hawk to and from competitions all over the state of California, and soon became even more involved. In 1980,

Street versus Vert

Inside the world of skateboarding there is a very real rivalry between two camps: street skaters and vertical skaters. Street skating is done on any surface or any structure found in the urban landscape, including parking lots, handrails, benches, or curbs. Vertical skating is performed on vertical ramps or other structures built specifically for the sport. Street skating came first, coming to light in the late 1970s in California with surfers executing dangerous stunts on the curved walls of empty swimming pools. There were no competitions with prize money, and skaters did not wear expensive designer duds. Street skaters considered themselves to be hip rebels, outside the mainstream.

Street-style skaters are still very much present in the 2000s. According to skateboarding insiders, as reported in *Sports Illustrated,* there are between 350 and 400 street skaters who are considered to be professionals, some of them as young as sixteen. They earn their reputations the old-fashioned way, performing outrageous tricks, without safety gear, in out-of-the-way, illegal places. Although they consider themselves to be "outlaws," many of them make a living from skateboarding. Just like Hawk, they get contracts from skateboard apparel and accessory companies, and they can bring home anywhere from $1,000 to $5,000 a month.

However, diehard street skaters do not appreciate the spotlight that Tony Hawk has turned on skateboarding. Many accuse him of selling out to corporate America and watering down what was once an edgy sport. Darrell Stanton, a teenage pro street skater who spoke with *Sports Illustrated,* echoed that sentiment: "I hope the whole skateboarding popularity thing stops before it gets too mainstream. I'd like for it to stay a raw sport." But statistics suggest that Stanton is unlikely to get his wish. According to the polling company American Sports Data, Inc., in 2003 more kids under the age of eighteen were skating than playing baseball.

dissatisfied by the quality of the competitions and the lack of sponsoring organizations, Frank Hawk founded the California Amateur Skateboard League (CASL). Three years later, in 1983, he established the National Skateboarding Association (NSA), the first professional skateboarding organization of its kind. Ultimately the high-profile events put on by the NSA were credited with boosting the popularity of skateboarding in the 1980s.

The biggest boost, however, came in the form of Tony Hawk himself. By age fourteen Hawk had turned professional, joining the Powell Peralta skateboard team called the Bones Brigade. By age sixteen he was dominating the sport. The road, however, was not an easy one. As Hawk won competition after competition, some veteran skaters cried favoritism, since his father was the NSA president. They also dismissed his wild, crazy skating as showboating. But that same creative skating gave birth to the Ollie, which became one of the most important moves in vertical skating. It also helped Hawk win three NSA championships and almost twenty additional pro events by the time he was eighteen.

A skateboard slump

Before he graduated from Torrey Pines High School in 1986, Hawk was earning $100,000 a year from skating in competitions, making public appearances, and endorsing products such as Mountain Dew. Known as the Birdman because of his high-flying acrobatics, he was also a featured performer in Bones Brigade videos, which to this day are watched by would-be skaters. Hawk bought his first house just before graduation, and as he told the *New York Times,* "That was an inkling that [skateboarding] was already my career."

By the end of the 1980s skateboarding was a hot sport, and Hawk was its king. But, like all things, popularity goes in cycles, and in the 1990s the public's interest in skateboarding had begun to wane. Part of the problem was the high cost of insurance required to run competitions and maintain skateparks. As a result, competitions were cancelled and skateparks around the United States were closed. This signaled disaster for Hawk, who now had very little money coming in, and a wife and child to support. In 1990 he had married his first wife, Cindy; two years later the couple had a son, Riley. His career sport was losing popularity, and a worried Hawk considered getting a regular nine-to-five job, possibly in computers, since he was a self-proclaimed techno geek. "I did demos where I could count the spectators on two hands," he recalled to Tim Layden of *Sports Illustrated.*

Instead, Hawk decided to throw himself into a new business venture. In 1990 he and fellow skateboarder Per Welinder launched Birdhouse Projects, a company to manufacture skateboards and skate accessories. In 1992 Birdhouse was followed by Blitz, which distributed other skateboard brands. Hawk mortgaged and eventually sold his home in order to finance his businesses. The rocky start-up proved to be too much of a strain on his family, however, and Tony and Cindy divorced. But just when it seemed that things could not get any worse, skateboarding once again came to the rescue.

Back in the game

In 1995 Hawk got a call from executives at the television sports network ESPN, who asked him to skate in a new alternative competition called X Games (Extreme Games). A more-than-interested Hawk flew to Rhode Island, where the contest was being held, and took first place in the vertical competition and second place in street skating. The televised event was seen by millions of people, and almost overnight the interest in skateboarding was re-ignited, as well as interest in Hawk and his career. Soon he was again "hawking" products on television, appearing in countless commercials for companies such as Coca-Cola, Pepsi, and Campbell's Soup. He also hosted a number of sports specials, including MTV's *Sports and Music Festival.*

Of course, Hawk also pumped up his skateboarding. He traveled around the world to skate in exhibitions, and year after year he swept the X Games, taking home both singles and doubles titles. By 1999 the king was back on his throne. During the 1999 X Games, Hawk made history during the Best Trick event, when he introduced a move called the 900, a move so spectacular and dangerous that no one has successfully landed it since. The 900 is a two-and-a-half rotation mid-air flip above the lip of the vertical ramp. Hawk had been working on the move for more than a decade, and had been seriously injured along the way. Landing the 900 was a personal triumph. As Hawk explained to Rose, "I just felt this great sense of relief that I'd finally conquered this beast that had plagued me for so long."

After the 900, it seemed that Hawk could do no wrong, especially in business, where he became a one-man marketing phenomenon. Birdhouse and Blitz took off, becoming two of the largest skateboarding companies in the world. In 1999, however, Hawk ventured into what would become his most lucrative enterprise—video games. He had been trying to interest companies in a skateboarding game since the mid-1990s, but executives did not bite. "They just didn't get it," Hawk explained to *Sports Illustrated.* Finally Activision, a California-based company, approached Hawk in September of 1998 about developing a video game. Computer engineers mocked up a working version and Hawk tinkered with it for months, providing feedback and offering suggestions for improvement. When Tony Hawk's Pro Skater was introduced in the fall of 1999, it created an immediate buzz. By Christmas it had zoomed to the top of the video sales charts.

In 2004 Activison released the fourth version of Pro Skater and added Tony Hawk's Underground to its catalog of games. Each game sold better than the last, and the Hawk series became one of the best-selling video lines of all time, with worldwide yearly sales in the hundreds of millions of dollars. Eager to cash in on Hawk's obvious appeal, more businesses lined up to strike deals. In 2000 the skateboarder became the spokesman for Hot Bites frozen snack foods. Hawk went on to lend his name to a slew of products, including toys, shoes, clothing, and DVDs. His most recent endorsement deals, which were reportedly worth over $1 million each, included McDonald's, Hershey's chocolate milk, and Frito Lay snacks. According to Jake Phelps, editor of *Thrasher* magazine (a skateboard magazine), who spoke with Layden, "Tony Hawk means ka-ching."

Boom Boom Huck Jam

Analysts have attributed Hawk's success to several factors. First, even in his thirties he continues to be one of the most talented skateboarders to ever hit the vertical ramp. Second, because of his many personal appearances, he is accessible to his fans. For example, every summer Hawk goes on a multi-city skateboarding tour with members of his Birdhouse team. For those who cannot make it to see Hawk in person, his tours are televised as ESPN specials. Third, according to marketers, Hawk has a squeaky-clean image and is viewed as the perfect family man, which makes him appealing not only to kids but to their parents. In 1999 Hawk remarried; he and his second wife, Erin, have two sons, Spencer and Keegan. All three of the Hawk boys seem to be following in their father's footsteps, and Riley, the oldest, has been skating since he was four.

Perhaps the biggest reason for Hawk's success, however, is that he remains passionate about the sport he picked up when he was a child. He still skates every day and, although he claims to be retired, he continues to compete in the X Games. In addition, Hawk is determined to grow the sport even further. One way to do that is through the Tony Hawk brainchild, Boom Boom Huck Jam, an annual event that combines rock music and extreme sports. As Hawk explained to Devin Gordon of *Newsweek,* "'Hucking' refers to launching in the air. 'Jam' is a gathering of talent. And 'boom boom' is just to give it some flavor." The ninety-minute spectacle was unveiled in 2002 in Las

Tony Hawk skates at the Edwards Air Force Base skatepark in California, in 2004. AP/Wide World Photos. Reproduced by permission.

Vegas, Nevada, and featured the best skateboarders, BMX bikers, and motocrossers in the world. Fans were also entertained by some of the hottest new bands around, including The Offspring and Good Charlotte. Following the Las Vegas unveiling, the whole ensemble took off on a 24-city North America tour, performing to sellout crowds.

Boom Boom Huck Jam is introducing a whole new generation of kids to skateboarding, but Hawk also wants to make sure that every kid who wants to skate has a chance. In 2002 he established the Tony Hawk Foundation, which provides money to help build and promote skateparks in low-income urban centers throughout the United States.

Since its inception the foundation has given assistance to more than 125 skateparks across the country.

Favorite male athlete

Hawk has endured many on-the-job hazards, including a broken elbow, cracked ribs, more sprains and scrapes than he can count, and multiple lost teeth. On the other hand, he has become a multi-million-aire and a living legend, all from riding on a board with wheels. A real pioneer of skateboarding, Hawk invented nearly one hundred tricks and moves that have been handed down to young skaters today. More important, he continues to serve as a role model and inspiration for children who consider him to be one of their all-time favorite sports stars. In fact, in the early 2000s, Hawk consistently topped most teen polls. For example, in 2003 and 2004 he was named Favorite Male Athlete at the Nickelodeon Kids' Choice Awards. All this, however, is just icing on the cake for Hawk. As he explained to *Sports Illustrated*: "Here's what skateboarding is to me. It's my form of exercise, my sport, my means of expression since I was nine years old. It's what I love. I never expected it to give me anything more than that."

For More Information

Books

Hawk, Tony, with Sean Mortimer. *Hawk: Occupation: Skateboarder.* New York, ReganBooks, 2002.

Periodicals

Ault, Susanne. "Hawk Splices Games, Music, Sports for HuckJam." *Billboard* (September 28, 2002): p. 16.

Givens, Ron. "Skateboarding's Best Seller." *New York Times Upfront* (December 11, 2000): p. 20.

Gordon, Devin. "Newsmakers: Tony Hawk." *Newsweek* (October 14, 2002): p. 71.

Layden, Tim. "What Is This 34-Year-Old Man Doing On A Skateboard? Making Millions." *Sports Illustrated* (June 10, 2002): pp. 80+.

Web Sites

Rose, Charlie. "Tony Hawk Takes Off." *CBSNews.com: 60 Minutes* (June 16, 2004). http://www.cbsnews.com/stories/2002/12/10/60II/main 532506.shtml (accessed on June 21, 2004).

Tony Hawk Official Web site. http://www.tonyhawk.com (accessed on June 21, 2004).

Saddam Hussein

AP/Wide World Photos. Reproduced by permission.

April 28, 1937 • Tikrit, Iraq

Former president of Iraq

Beginning in the 1970s, Saddam Hussein ruled the Republic of Iraq with a tight grip. His supporters maintained that through his many social and economic programs he effectively brought the country into the modern age. His many critics, however, claimed that Saddam was a ruthless dictator who would stop at nothing in his endless push for power. Regardless, the charismatic leader retained control of his country during countless military conflicts, including an eight-year war against Iran in the 1980s and the Persian Gulf War in 1991. He also survived a slew of assassination attempts throughout the course of his presidency, and at times he seemed almost invincible. But in March of 2003, U.S.-led forces invaded Iraq and deposed the defiant leader. Saddam escaped capture, but after a nine-month manhunt, he was caught, imprisoned, and faced multiple charges relating to war crimes and human rights abuses. Many speculated that the once-invincible ruler would ultimately face the death penalty.

A troubled beginning

The ex-president of Iraq had a troubled childhood. Saddam Hussein was born on April 28, 1937, in the village of Al-Awja, near Tikrit, a town just north of the city of Baghdad, in central Iraq. His father, Hussein 'Abd al-Majid, was a peasant sheepherder who by various accounts either died or disappeared before his son's birth. His older brother, who was twelve, died of cancer shortly thereafter. The combined tragedies had a devastating effect on Saddam's mother, Subha Tulfah al-Mussallat, who became extremely depressed during her last months of pregnancy. After her new son was born, she named him Saddam, which means "one who confronts" or "the stubborn one." Because of her depression, however, she was unable

> **"**We are ready to sacrifice our souls, our children, and our families so as not to give up Iraq. We say this so no one will think that America is capable of breaking the will of the Iraqis with its weapons.**"**

to care for him, and young Saddam was sent to live in Baghdad with his uncle, Khairallah Talfah, a retired army officer and Arab nationalist.

When he was three years old Saddam returned to live with his mother, but she had remarried and family life was not pleasant. His new stepfather was abusive and treated him harshly over the next several years. As a result, when he was ten years old Saddam ran away to the safety of his uncle's home. Khairallah Talfah served as a role model for his nephew, especially influencing his political beliefs. After Saddam graduated from the al-Karh Secondary School in Baghdad, he officially joined his uncle's political party, the Arab Baa'th Socialist Party, which had been formed in Syria in 1947 with the goal of promoting unity among the various Arab states in the Middle East. In Iraq and neighboring countries the Baa'th Party had become an underground revolutionary force.

In 1959, when Saddam was just twenty-two years old, he played a major part in the assassination attempt of Iraqi Prime Minister Abdul Karim Qassim by the Baa'th Party. He was shot in the leg but managed to escape, first to Syria and then to Cairo, Egypt. While in Egypt he studied law at the University of Cairo. In 1963, after a military overthrow of Qassim's government, Saddam was allowed to return to Iraq. That same year he married his first wife, Sajida, the daughter of his mentor, Khairallah Talfah. His return was short-lived, however, since internal squabbling within the new Baa'th regime led to its downfall. Once again Saddam was forced into hiding, but he was caught in 1964 and imprisoned for the next two years. Although in jail, he remained involved in party politics. Escaping from prison in 1966, Saddam became a rising star in the Baa'th organization, forming close ties with key party officials who were planning a second attempt at taking control of Iraq.

In July of 1968 the Baa'ths organized a successful takeover of the Iraqi government. Ahmed Hassan al-Bakr, a retired general and prominent party spokesman who was a distant relative of Saddam, assumed the role of chairman of the Baa'th Revolutionary Command Council (RCC) as well as the presidency of Iraq. Saddam, who had become an integral part of the organization, was named vice president.

Second in command

Although Ahmed Hassan was officially the president of Iraq from 1969 through 1979, it was Saddam Hussein who truly held the reins. And thanks to Saddam, the country enjoyed its most stable and productive period in recent history. After oil prices soared in the 1970s (oil is Iraq's primary natural resource and export), he used the revenues to institute a major system of economic reform and launched an array of wide-ranging social programs. Roads were paved, hospitals and schools were built, and various types of industry, such as mining, were expanded. In particular, Saddam focused attention on the rural areas, where roughly two-thirds of the population lived. Land was brought under the control of the Iraqi government, which meant that large properties were broken up and parcels distributed to small farmers. Saddam also funneled revenues into modernizing the country's agriculture industry. For example, he brought electricity into even some of the most remote communities.

Saddam's social programs benefited both rural and city dwellers. In an effort to wipe out illiteracy, he established free schooling for children through high school and made it a government requirement that all children attend school. Saddam's government also provided free hospitalization to all Iraqis and gave full economic support to families of Iraqi soldiers. Such large-scale social programs were unheard of in any other Middle Eastern country.

When he created his massive reforms, Saddam may have had the benefit of his people in mind, but he was also a shrewd politician. In order to maintain a stable government and to assure that his party would remain in power, it was necessary to gather as much support as possible. By the late 1970s the Baa'th regime enjoyed a widespread following among the working classes, and the party was firmly unified around its second-in-command. Saddam also served as the outward face of the Iraqi government, representing the nation on both the domestic and international fronts. On July 22, 1979, when an ailing Ahmed Hassan al-Bakr decided to step down as president, it came as no surprise that Saddam Hussein stepped into his shoes.

The cult of Saddam Hussein

Support for Saddam Hussein was not universal. The conservative followers of Islam (the national religion of Iraq) did not agree with many of Saddam's innovations, which they felt were directly opposed to Islamic law. This included legislation that gave women more freedoms and the fact that a Western-style legal system had been installed. As a result, Iraq became the only Arab country not ruled by the laws of Islam. Major opposition also came from the Kurds who occupied the northern region of the country. The Kurds are a nomadic people who are concentrated in areas of Turkey, Iran, and Iraq. They are Muslim but not Arabic, and they strongly disagreed with the Baa'thist push for a united Arab front.

Saddam even faced resistance within his own party, and he made it a policy to weed out anyone he viewed as a threat. On July 22, 1979, just days after taking over the presidency, he organized an assembly of Baa'th leaders and read aloud the names of suspected spies; these people were taken from the room and publicly executed by firing squad. A few years later, in 1982, he ordered the execution of

Tiled portrait of Saddam Hussein in Tikrit, Iraq. Many such images and statues of Hussein appeared in cities throughout Iraq. © Shepard Sherbell/Corbis.

at least three hundred officers who had supposedly questioned his military tactics. Once in control, Saddam surrounded himself with a tightly-knit group of family and friends who assumed high levels of responsibility within the government. These individuals, however, were not necessarily immune to Saddam's paranoia. At one point, Adnan Talfah, Saddam's brother-in-law and childhood friend, was killed in a "mysterious" helicopter crash. And in 1996 Saddam had his sons-in-law murdered for being disloyal.

Although he ruled with an iron fist, Saddam also was preoccupied with winning the devotion of the Iraqi people. He promoted himself as a hero of the nation who was dedicated to making Iraq the leader of the Arab world. Images of Saddam were plastered throughout the country. Some of them depicted the ruler as a dedicated Muslim wearing traditional robes and headdress; others featured Saddam in a Western-style business suit, wearing sunglasses and holding a rifle over his head. All were efforts to make a connection at every level of society and to solidify his role as an all-powerful president.

Such tactics, however, also solidified his reputation as an insecure and unstable leader. He became known for his paranoia, which was not unjustified, considering he had survived at least seven assassination attempts. As a result he rarely appeared in public. He also slept only a few hours a night, at secret locations, and all of his food was carefully prepared and inspected by official food tasters.

Conflicts with Iran and Kuwait

Outside of Iraq, especially in the West, Saddam was seen as a dictator whose quest for dominance in the Middle East was viewed with particular concern. In 1980 Saddam proved that such fears were founded when he attacked Iran, an invasion that led to an eight-year bloody conflict. Relations between Iran and Iraq had been deteriorating for years, and came to a head in 1979 when the Ayatollah Khomeini (c. 1900–1989) overthrew the government of Iran during an Islamic uprising. Saddam worried that Khomeini would set his sites on spreading his radical religious rule to the secular (nonreligious) state of Iraq. Disputes over territorial boundaries led to skirmishes throughout late 1979 and into 1980, and on September 22, 1980, Iraqi forces crossed the Iranian border and officially declared war.

Over the next eight years, both countries suffered almost irreparable damage, and the healthy economy that Saddam had created during the 1970s was in ruins. Billions of dollars were borrowed from countries such as the United States, Kuwait, the U.S.S.R., and France, to support the war effort. The United States alone gave the Iraqi government nearly $40 billion in food supplies and arms. And both sides suffered a tremendous loss of human life. It is estimated that approximately 1.7 million people were killed during the conflict. In one battle on March 16, 1988, Iraqi troops attacked the Kurdish town of Halabja, using poison nerve gas. Nearly five thousand people died, most of whom were women and children. Various reports claimed that chemical weapons were used by both Iran and Iraq, but these tactics continued to raise the alarm that Saddam Hussein was a military threat who could not be trusted.

In 1989 the war ended in a stalemate, with no side claiming a real victory. Conflicts between Saddam and other nations, however, were just beginning. Faced with the prospect of rebuilding his country, Saddam tried to pressure the neighboring country of Kuwait to forgive the $30 billion loan he had been given. The reason he gave was that the war with Iran had effectively protected Kuwait from an Iranian invasion. Tensions were also sparked between the two countries over territorial boundaries that were especially important because they involved the control of oil reserves in the area. When negotiations failed, Saddam invaded Kuwait on August 2, 1990.

The unprovoked attack was denounced by governments throughout the world, especially the United States. The administration of Ronald Reagan (1911–2004) in the 1980s may have seen Saddam as a potential ally, but after the invasion of Kuwait, President George H. W. Bush (1924–) essentially severed all ties between the United States and Saddam Hussein. As a result, when the Iraqi leader refused to leave Kuwait, a combined force of U.S. and United Nations (UN) troops stepped in. Fighting lasted a mere six weeks, but after the Persian Gulf War came to an end, casualties topped over eighty-five thousand. Saddam was successfully evicted from Kuwait, but the tensions were not over. Bush ordered U.S. troops to protect Kuwaiti borders, and in his March of 1991 State of the Union address he told the American people, "We all realize that our responsibility to be the catalyst for peace in the region does not end with the successful conclusion of this war." He called Saddam a brutal dictator "who will do anything, will use any weapon, will commit any outrage, no matter how many innocents suffer."

The United States versus Iraq

In an effort to control Saddam, the cease-fire agreement drawn up between the United Nations and Iraq required the country to destroy all of its chemical, nuclear, and biological weapons. The agreement also stipulated that Saddam had to let UN inspectors oversee the efforts. If Iraq did not comply with the agreement, economic sanctions would be imposed, meaning that all trade with the country would be cut off. Throughout the 1990s the Iraqi leader reportedly concealed the manufacture of weapons from inspectors, and the sanctions continued. Cut off from the world, the people of Iraq suffered. Unemployment rose, agricultural production declined, and the majority of the population suffered from severe malnutrition and lack of medical care. There was increased unrest among the many factions in the country, which prompted Saddam to increase his tactics of repression.

When George W. Bush became president of the United States in 2001, one of his first acts upon taking office was an attempt to reinstate economic sanctions, which had been lifted by the United Nations in the late 1990s. World opinion opposed the effort as inhumane; the Iraqi people had suffered far too much. Anti-Saddam sentiment only escalated, however, after the terrorist attacks of September 11, 2001. Although the attacks were never linked to Saddam Hussein, Bush insisted that terrorists armed with Iraqi weapons could at any time target the United States. In his State of the Union address in January of 2002, the U.S. president called Iraq part of an "axis of evil," and claimed that the country "continue[d] to flaunt its hostility toward America and to support terror."

Time and again Bush publicly accused Saddam of concealing weapons, and by 2002 he threatened to invade Iraq if UN inspectors were not allowed back into the country. Saddam countered that there were no weapons, and opened his doors. Although UN inspectors found nothing, Bush maintained that inspectors had simply not found the well-hidden weapons yet. By early 2003, war with Iraq was looming. In January of 2003 Bush gave Saddam an ultimatum: either totally disarm his country or voluntarily leave Iraq. If neither step was taken, the United States would attack.

In February of 2003, in an unprecedented move, Saddam Hussein appeared on television, having agreed to be interviewed by CBS newsman Dan Rather (1931–). The interview was broadcast worldwide, even in Iraq, which meant that the Iraqi people were given a rare glimpse of their reclusive leader who was rarely seen in person. Saddam accused the Bush administration of being part of a "bandwagon of evil," and continued to insist that Iraq did not have concealed weapons and that it had nothing to do with the September 11 attacks. He also explained that he would not leave Iraq and that Iraqis would fight to protect their country if provoked. "We will die here in Iraq," he told Rather. "We will die in this country and we will maintain our honor."

The Saddam regime is toppled

Despite massive international opposition, hundreds of thousands of U.S. and British troops stormed Iraq on March 20, 2003. Several air strikes specifically aimed at assassinating Saddam Hussein were unsuccessful, and ground troops pushed through the country, heading toward Baghdad, the capital of Iraq. In early April, just three weeks after the invasion, the Saddam regime was toppled. When Baghdad fell, however, the Iraqi president was nowhere to be found. Saddam managed to elude capture throughout the remainder of the year. Reports of Saddam sightings popped up occasionally, but proved to be false. In addition, audiotapes by the ousted leader were released to Arab television networks. Whether they were truly from Saddam remained in question.

High-ranking members of the Iraqi government were caught one by one, but Saddam remained at the top of the most-wanted list. In July of 2003 his two sons and political heirs, Uday and Qusay, were killed by U.S. forces. It was thought that perhaps Saddam's capture would be imminent, but the elusive leader remained on the run for the next five months. Finally, on December 13, 2003, Saddam Hussein was located just nine miles outside of his hometown of Tikrit, hiding in an underground cavern known as a "spider hole." Disheveled and dirty, with a graying beard and matted hair, he surrendered without resisting. According to commander of U.S. forces Lt. Gen. Ricardo Sanchez, as quoted on CNN.com, "He was a tired man. Also, I think, a man resigned to his fate."

The deposed leader was taken into custody by U.S. forces and held in Baghdad until June 30, 2004, when he was officially handed over to acting Iraqi government officials. On July 1 he faced his first legal hearing before an Iraqi Special Tribunal. During the twenty-six minute hearing he was charged with multiple crimes, including the 1988 attack on the Kurdish village of Halabja, the 1991 invasion of Kuwait, and the killings of political and religious leaders during his thirty years in command. Throughout the accusations Saddam remained defiant, claiming that the tribunal was a farce. He also maintained that he was still the true leader of Iraq. "I am Saddam Hussein al-Majid, the President of the Republic of Iraq," he announced, as quoted in England's *Guardian*. "I am still the president of the republic and the occupation cannot take that away."

Following the hearing Saddam remained in custody, where he reportedly spent time writing poetry, reading the Koran (the sacred writings of Islam), and tending to a small garden within the walls of his Baghdad prison. There were also reports that the sixty-seven-year-old former president was in poor health and that perhaps he had suffered a stroke. Such reports were denied by doctors. It seemed that Saddam would be well enough to face his accusers in a trial set to begin in January of 2005. Many speculated on the trial's outcome, but people in Iraq voiced their clear expectations. Shortly after U.S. forces turned Saddam Hussein over to Iraqi officials, the Iraqi government reinstated the death penalty, which had been temporarily suspended under U.S. occupation. Hamid al-Bayati, the deputy foreign minister of Iraq, was quoted in the *Guardian* as saying, "Everyone who lost loved ones to Saddam will want to see this."

For More Information

Books

"Saddam Hussein." In *Encyclopedia of World Biography.* 2nd ed. Detroit, MI: Gale Research, 1998.

Web Sites

McCallester, Matthew. "A Day in the Life of Saddam Hussein." *Indian Express* (July 27, 2004). http://www.indianexpress.com/full_story.php?content_id=51826 (accessed on August 3, 2004).

McCarthy, Rory. "I am Saddam Hussein, the President of Iraq." *Guardian* (England) (July 2, 2004). http://www.guardian.co.uk/international/story/0,,1252291,00.html (accessed on August 3, 2004).

"President George H. W. Bush's Address Before a Joint Session of the Congress on the State of the Union, January 29, 1991." *CSPAN.* http://www.c-span.org/executive/transcript.asp?cat=current_event&code=bush_admin&year=1991 (accessed on Augst 3, 2004).

"President George W. Bush's State of the Union Address to the Joint Session of Congress, January 29, 2002." *CSPAN Web site.* http://www.c-span.org/executive/transcript.asp?cat=current_event&code=bush_admin&year=2002 (accessed on August 3, 2003).

Rather, Dan. "Interview with Saddam Hussein." *CBS News* (February 24, 2003). http://www.cbsnews.com/stories/2003/02/24/eveningnews/main541817.shtml (accessed on August 3, 2004).

"The Rise and Fall of a Dictator." *CNN.com: World* (December 14, 2003). http://www.cnn.com/2003/WORLD/meast/12/14/sprj.irq.saddam.profile/index.html (accessed on August 2, 2004).

"Saddam Caught Like a Rat in a Hole." *CNN.com: World* (December 15, 2003). http://www.cnn.com/2003/WORLD/meast/12/14/sprj.irq.saddam.operation (accessed on August 2, 2003).

Hugh Jackman

AP/Wide World Photos. Reproduced by permission.

October 12, 1968 • *Sydney, Australia*

Actor

By the mid-2000s, the press was calling Australian actor Hugh Jackman a jack-of-all-trades. American moviegoers lined up to see him in the *X-Men* blockbusters, in which he played the ultimate alternative superhero: the brooding, razor-clawed mutant known as Wolverine. On the Broadway stage he received rave reviews for portraying flamboyant Australian song-and-dance-man Peter Allen in *The Boy from Oz*. In 2004 he landed a Tony Award, Broadway's most prestigious honor, for his role. Whether Jackman was wearing metal claws or clicking castanets, he earned praise from fans and critics alike. Jackman also added another term to his resume, that of America's favorite leading man.

From journalism to the stage

Hugh Jackman was born on October 12, 1968, the youngest of five Jackman children, and the only one born in Sydney, Australia. The entire family had moved to Australia from England in 1967, the year before his birth. When Jackman was eight years old his parents divorced. His mother returned to England to live and care for her own mother, who was ill; the job of taking care of the five young Jackmans fell to his father, an accountant. In interviews, Jackman cannot say enough about the man who devoted himself to his family. "He's an extraordinarily selfless, amazing man," Jackman remarked to Katie Couric on *MSNBC News*. Although his mother was not a part of his everyday life, Jackman did travel back and forth between Australia and England for visits. It was during those visits that he got his first taste of the theater.

"**I act because I have felt in acting some of the most free moments in my life.... I think it's also one thing that scares me the most.**"

Jackman loved going to plays with his mother, and he frequently acted in school plays, but he did not consider becoming a professional actor. Instead he majored in communications at the University of Technology in Sydney, with an eye toward journalism. During his senior year, Jackman found himself a few credits short, so he decided to take a drama class, primarily because his friends told him that he was guaranteed an easy "A." But as it turned out, the class was a lot of work. "I was shocked at how challenging it was," he admitted to *MSNBC News*. The class project was to put on a play, and everyone had to take a part. By chance Jackman was cast in the lead, and by the end of the term he was hooked.

After graduating with a bachelor's degree, Jackman realized that he was not truly cut out to be a journalist, so he enrolled at the Western Australia Academy of Performing Arts in Perth to study drama. The aspiring actor thrived in the experimental environment of the academy, where students were encouraged to work on instinct. As Jackman explained to David Furnish of *Interview,* "I studied in Perth, where you're totally isolated and in this bubble of creative fire and risk-taking." For the next three years Jackman immersed himself in

The X-Men and Wolverine

The *X-Men* series was created in 1963 by two Marvel Comics legends, writer Stan Lee (1922–) and artist Jack Kirby (1917–1994). The story originally focused on Professor Charles Xavier, who scoured the earth to find human beings who had been born with a genetic mutation that gave them each a special power. Xavier's goal was to provide a safe haven for the mutants, who were scorned and feared by society, and to help them harness their potentially dangerous gifts. The core group of X-Men consisted of five teenagers: Cyclops, Angel, Iceman, Beast, and Marvel Girl. The villain in the story was the evil Magneto, who believed that "normal" humans were inferior and had to be punished for their past treatment of mutants.

Since then, the series has undergone numerous transformations. Superheroes have been added and subtracted, villains have come and gone, and spin-offs have been created that concentrate on specific characters. One particularly popular character is Wolverine. Wolverine was created in 1974 by writer Len Wein because Marvel Comics had no Canadian superheroes. He was introduced in an Incredible Hulk comic as a secret agent of the Canadian government who had ultra-super powers. Several months after the Hulk comic was released, Wein was given the task of adding new characters to *The X-Men* series. As a result, Wolverine found a permanent home.

Wolverine is one of the toughest and most ruthless of the X-Men, and his mutant powers are many. He is incredibly strong and fast, and his keen sense of smell allows him to track almost any living creature. One of the most amazing things is that his skeleton has been infused with adamantium, a particularly strong, nearly indestructible metal. Wolverine has retractable claws built into the backs of his hands made from this metal. When the claws project through the skin of his hands, the flesh tears and bleeds, but because of Wolverine's self-healing powers, he mends quickly.

acting, appearing in plays and taking classes in opera and musical theater. When he graduated in 1994, he had no clear expectations for his future. As Jackman told Furnish, "After I graduated I thought, 'Well, I'm going to give this everything I've got for five years. If nothing happens, I'll start my own theater company or whatever.... I'm not going to spend my whole life waiting for the phone to ring.'"

Jackman did not have to wait by the phone for long. Almost immediately he was offered a plum role on the popular Australian television series *Corelli*. The program not only gave Jackman his first big break, it also gave him the chance to work opposite his future wife, Australian actress Deborra-Lee Furness. Following *Corelli*, Jackman appeared in a number of other TV shows. He also began to earn a reputation for his work on the stage in the Australian productions of *Beauty and the Beast* and *Sunset Boulevard*. In 1998 Jackman headed to London, where he drew even wider attention for his por-

trayal of singing cowboy Curly McClain in the Royal National The-
atre production of the musical *Oklahoma!* Critics and theater-goers
were so taken with Jackman's charming performance that he was
nominated for an Olivier. The Olivier Award is the most prestigious
theater honor in Great Britain, and is named for the renowned British
actor Sir Laurence Olivier (1907–1989).

Sharpens claws as Wolverine

Just a few short years out of drama school, Jackman had become the
hottest actor in Australia. He not only had television and stage credits
under his belt, he also found time to appear in two films, *Paperback
Heroes* and *Erskineville Kings,* both released in 1999. For his turn as
Wace in *Erskineville,* Jackman received a Best Actor nomination from
the Australian Film Institute. Although he did not take home the prize,
he was given an even bigger honor when he was named the Australian
Star of 1999.

Jackman may have been the biggest ticket in Australia, but he
was not big enough to be considered for an ambitious movie project
called *The X-Men* that was under way at Twentieth-Century Fox in the
United States. *The X-Men* movie was based on characters from a Marvel comic-book series of the same name, and although the characters
had legions of followers in the comic-book world, they were not well
known by the general public. Executives at Marvel and Fox, however,
felt the story had a timeless appeal, especially for a younger audience,
since it focused on the exploits of a group of outsiders who are
shunned because they are different. There was also the promise of a
special-effects spectacular, because what made the X-Men different
was that each was born with a special power. For example, Cyclops
can fire beams of energy from his eyes.

The character slated to be at the center of the movie was
Wolverine, a shaggy mutant with keen animal senses and razor-sharp
metal claws that spring from his hands. British actor Dougray Scott
(1965–) was Hollywood's first choice to play the brooding Wolverine,
but when another film obligation got in the way he was forced to back
out. This left the studio in a bind just as the movie was about to begin
shooting in October of 1999. Director Bryan Singer decided to take a
gamble and tapped newcomer Jackman to replace Scott. When Jack-

man received the call he was stunned, especially since he had auditioned for the role ten months earlier. As he laughingly told Lori Blackman of *CNN.com,* "I think I'm in the record books for the longest audition in history."

The gamble paid off when *The X-Men* far exceeded everyone's expectations. There was a buzz about the movie months before its debut, and comic-book fans, eager to finally see their favorite superheroes on the big screen, camped out in front of theaters to get tickets. When the film was released in July of 2000, it took in a record-breaking $57 million during its opening weekend, and by the time it went to DVD, worldwide ticket sales totalled almost $300 million. The movie also spawned a lucrative marketing franchise that included video games and action figures. By 2001, it looked like superheroes meant super business.

Big-budget star

In the process Hugh Jackman became an overnight celebrity. Diehard *X-Men* fans praised Jackman for his faithful portrayal of Wolverine. This was quite a compliment, considering the fact that the fictional Wolverine stands five-foot three inches tall, and Jackman is over six feet tall. In addition, Jackman's chiseled good looks and mutton-chop sideburns made him America's newest heartthrob.

Studios lined up to sign the hunky Australian, and in 2001 Jackman had a banner year, appearing in no less than three movies, including *Swordfish,* a suspense drama starring John Travolta (1954–). He also co-starred opposite Meg Ryan (c. 1961–) as a time-traveling suitor in *Kate & Leopold,* and he played the object of Ashley Judd's (1968–) affections in *Someone Like You.* Jackman performed admirably in all three films, especially in *Kate & Leopold,* where he proved he could handle a romantic comedy as well as an action-packed thriller. None of the movies did well at the box office, however, and critics considered the films to be fairly forgettable.

In 2003 it seemed to many that Jackman was back where he belonged when he reprised his role as Wolverine in the *X-Men* sequel, *X2: X-Men United.* The movie not only repeated the success of the original *X-Men,* raking in an astonishing $85 million during its opening weekend, it was also considered by most critics to be even better than the original. Jackman, as Wolverine, was given a lot of the credit even though he was just one of an ensemble cast.

Jackman was believed to be such an integral part of the big-budget fantasy's success that writer-director Stephen Sommers created a movie called *Van Helsing* specifically for him. As Sommers told Benjamin Svetkey of *Entertainment Weekly,* "I wrote *Van Helsing* with Jackman in mind. I'm not sure what I would have done if he had said no." But Jackman did not say no. He jumped at the chance to play monster-hunter Gabriel Van Helsing, who, in his sweeping duster and broad-brimmed hat, pursues the likes of Dracula, Frankenstein's monster, and the Wolf Man. When *Van Helsing* opened in May of 2004, it received mixed reviews. Some critics dismissed it as "summer silliness," but they also gave kudos to Jackman for his intense performance. Many, like Leah Rozen of *People,* wondered when the actor was "going to get a movie worthy of his true talent."

The Boy from Oz

Jackman claimed that taking the Van Helsing role was part of his plan to further his career. As he explained to Svetkey, it was a way to "make sure the projects kept getting more and more interesting and the parts more and more challenging." If some questioned his choice of playing the part of a monster-killer, others questioned Jackman's choice in 2003—performing on Broadway in *The Boy from Oz,* a musical about the life and death of singer-songwriter Peter Allen (1944–1992). But Jackman was itching to flex his acting muscles, and Allen was an Australian legend. As Jackman explained to Furnish, "[Allen] may not have been the greatest singer or piano player or dancer in the world, but when he performed, he just lit up the stage."

Beginning in September of 2003, Jackman himself lit up the stage in *The Boy from Oz,* singing twenty-one songs per show in eight shows per week. Those who had known Allen were amazed by Jackman's uncanny ability to capture the essence of the exuberant showman. The resemblance was particularly noticeable when Jackman, like Allen, interacted with his audience. For example, during one performance Jackman was interrupted by some latecomers, so he strayed from the script and chatted with the ladies, ultimately forcing them to

Hugh Jackman poses with his 2004 Tony Award. AP/Wide World Photos. Reproduced by permission.

stand up and show off their outfits. When an actor ad-libs, it can be a disaster, but Phil McKinley, the *Oz* director, called Jackman a dream to work with. And he predicted great things for his leading man. "Hugh's going to have this amazing career where he truly will be an all-around superstar performer," McKinley commented to *MSNBC News*.

Although critics were not particularly kind to the show, Jackman received the highest marks for his demanding role. He also generated an enormous following. A group of devoted fans, who called themselves the Ozalots, went to see him perform twenty or thirty times in a row. By June of 2004, Jackman had created such a stir that it came as no surprise when he won the Tony Award for Best Actor in a Musical.

Time with Oscar

In October of 2004, when the run of *The Boy from Oz* ended, Jackman was only too eager to take a break. As he told Katie Couric, his plans were simple: "As soon as I finish … I'm going to just hang out with Oscar." Oscar is Jackman's young son. He also explained that he might find time to fit in some gardening and cooking. Not the most adventurous schedule for a man known for playing dynamic characters on stage and screen, or for the fellow who consistently makes *People* magazine's "50 Most Beautiful People" list. But those who know Jackman have described him as very relaxed and down-to-earth. That may be because he has studied philosophy for more than ten years, and Jackman has claimed that this helps him put his fame into perspective. As he told Furnish, "My studies have helped me…. To see the roller-coaster quality [of fame]. I mean, success in this business is very much determined by public opinion, and we all know how fickle that can be."

For More Information

Periodicals

Furnish, David. "Hugh Jackman: From an X-Man to a Song and Dance Man, Hugh Jackman is Redefining the Words 'Leading Man.'" *Interview* (May 2004): pp. 98–104.

Scott, A. O. "Full Moon, Romance, and a Demon Rustler." Review of *Van Helsing*. *New York Times* (May 7, 2004).

Svetkey, Benjamin. "Monster, Inc. Hugh Jackman Pursues Gruesome Creatures—and the Summer's First Smash—with Van Helsing." *Entertainment Weekly* (March 26, 2004): p. 22.

Web Sites

"Big Tony Winners." *CBS News: The Early Show* (June 8, 2004). http://www.cbsnews.com/stories/2004/06/07/earlyshow/leisure/main621619.shtml (accessed on June 24, 2004).

Blackman, Lori. "'Wolverine' Hugh Jackman" *CNN.com: Showbiz Today* (July 19, 2000). http://www.cnn.com/2000/SHOWBIZ/Movies/07/19/sbtst.jackman/index.html (accessed on June 24, 2004).

"Comics: The X-Men." *Marvel Enterprises Web site.* http://www.marvel.com/publishing/showcomic.htm?id=4 (accessed on June 30, 2004).

Couric, Katie. "Hugh Jack(Man) of All Trades." *MSNBC News: Dateline NBC* (May 7, 2004). http://www.msnbc.msn.com/id/4925357 (accessed on June 24, 2004).

"Hugh Jackman Relishes Performing." *MSNBC News: Entertainment* (May 11, 2004). http://www.msnbc.msn.com/id/4893079 (accessed on June 24, 2004).

"Hugh Jackman's Big Year." *CBS News: The Early Show* (June 4, 2004). http://www.cbsnews.com/stories/2004/06/03/earlyshow/leisure/celeb-spot/main620969.shtml (accessed on June 24, 2004).

Peter Jackson

AP/Wide World Photos. Reproduced by permission.

October 31, 1961 • *Pukerua Bay, North Island, New Zealand*

Filmmaker

Peter Jackson made a name for himself in the movie industry with a small collection of gory, low-budget horror films including *Dead Alive* and *The Frighteners*. He worked from his native New Zealand, more than six thousand miles from Hollywood. To many, Jackson may have seemed like the least likely person to be chosen to direct one of the most lavish and big-budgeted film projects ever attempted. He may have seemed even less likely to succeed in such a venture, but succeed he did, in grand style. Jackson spent seven years of his life creating the three *Lord of the Rings* films, which are based on the beloved classic fantasy novels by J. R. R. Tolkien (1892–1973). Each installment of the trilogy earned the devotion of millions of fans, close to $1 billion worldwide at the box office, and multiple award nominations. With the final film, *Lord of the Rings: Return of the King,* Jackson hit the award jackpot. The film swept the 2004 Academy Awards with eleven victories, including best director, best adapted screenplay, and best picture. With these three films, Jackson went from being a filmmaker admired by a select group of fans to one who is regarded by many as one of the world's top directors.

An active imagination

Jackson was born in 1961 on Halloween, October 31, an appropriate birthday for a boy who would grow up to make exceptionally scary, blood-soaked films. Growing up an only child in a town near Wellington, New Zealand, he found his imagination fired by watching such television shows as *Monty Python's Flying Circus* and *Batman,* and old monster movies like the 1933 version of *King Kong.* At the age of

> **"**To me [the *Lord of the Rings* trilogy] embodies what I love about movies. I love movies for their escapism, for the fact that you go into the cinema and you just give yourself over to the film and allow it to sweep you away.**"**

eight, Jackson began playing around with his parents' 8-millimeter camera, making home movies. At age twelve, he and some friends shot a short World War II film, using Jackson's backyard as the set. Perplexed as to how to create realistic gunfire in the film, Jackson hit upon the idea of making holes in the strip of film in the frames where the guns would be fired; when the film was projected, the holes appeared as a flash onscreen. This special effect was the first of many Jackson would create throughout his career: as a filmmaker he became famous for his elaborate, complicated special effects.

When Jackson was seventeen years old, he left school to find a job in New Zealand's movie industry. To support himself, he took a job as an apprentice, a beginner learning a trade, in the photo-engraving department of a newspaper, the *Evening Post.* Among his first purchases once he started receiving paychecks was a used 16-millimeter

The Creation of Gollum

Many of the computer-generated creatures in Peter Jackson's *The Lord of the Rings* trilogy have incredibly lifelike features. They seem to live and breathe, in some cases to think and feel. One such creature, Gollum, exhibits as much emotion and complexity as any of the human actors, and for that, actor Andy Serkis (1964–) is responsible. In a unique pairing of human performance and computer-generated images, or CGI, Jackson hired Serkis to provide not just the voice of Gollum, but the creature's facial expressions and body movements as well.

In the films, which depict the long and painful journey of the hobbit Frodo to destroy the One Ring, a ring that makes its bearer all-powerful and must be destroyed to prevent its misuse, Gollum is a deformed, stooped, hairless creature who once was a ring-bearer like Frodo. He began life as a hobbit named Smeagol, and his years possessing the ring corrupted him in both mind and body. Gollum joins Frodo and his friend Sam for a portion of their journey, longing to steal back the ring, which he calls "my Precious."

Serkis originally agreed to the role of Gollum thinking it would involve a few weeks of voice-over work. He told Michael Fleming of *Daily Variety,* "I remember thinking, a voice-over? Why can't I get offered a decent acting role in a major movie? … This didn't seem that involved." He soon realized, however, that his contributions to the character would go far beyond Gollum's reptile-like hissings. By the end of the three films' production, Serkis had worked more hours than any other actor in the films. And his extraordinary contributions brought him high praise from critics and fans, with many suggesting he should be nominated for an Academy Award for his performance.

Serkis began by acting out the role of Gollum with his costars, creating the character's physical style. Animators observed Serkis's performance, using his movements as the basis for the Gollum they created on computers. Serkis then went through each of Gollum's scenes again, this time wearing a high-tech motion-capture suit. Sensors covering the suit transmitted details about Serkis's every move to the animators' computers, enabling the graphic artists to digitally recreate Serkis's physical motions with startling accuracy. Serkis performed his scenes a third time to capture Gollum's voice and to give the animators a starting point for Gollum's facial expressions. A team of forty animators then spent untold hours refining the creature's movements. At Serkis's Web site, the films' creature supervisor, Eric Sainden, explained the complexity of the computer-generated Gollum: "There are around 300 different muscles or more on Gollum. He has a full skeleton and a full muscle system that's all driving what you see on his skin…. The facial system we're doing has about 250 different face shapes…." The result is a believable, realistic Gollum, what Peter Jackson described at Serkis's Web site as "probably the most actor-driven digital creature that has ever been used in a film before."

For Serkis, his months of work creating Gollum have yielded an unusual legacy, summed up in *Daily Variety:* "The performance is signature Serkis—even though the actor was erased from every scene."

camera. Soon, with the help of some friends, Jackson had begun making a short film about aliens from outer space who dine on human flesh. He spent weekends and holidays for several years working on this film, spending his own money to finance it. It eventually became clear that the film, titled *Bad Taste,* would be a full-length effort. Jackson cowrote the film and served as director, producer, cinematographer, editor, make-up artist, and even actor. He also served as fundraiser, successfully applying to the New Zealand Film Commission for a grant to complete post-production work. When the movie was completed, the commission felt enough confidence in it to take it to the prestigious Cannes Film Festival in France. Audiences there reacted strongly, some loving it and some despising it. However, even its detractors could see evidence of a unique, talented filmmaker. As Stephen Rebello of *Variety* wrote in 2003: "Wade through the spilled guts, shove aside the cracked skull and exploding sheep in 1987's *Bad Taste,* and you're bound to see the flair of its twenty-six-year-old director." *Bad Taste* was sold for distribution in thirty countries, giving Jackson a big enough paycheck to allow him to quit his job at the newspaper and become a full-time filmmaker.

A blood-spattered film catalog

At a screening for *Bad Taste,* Jackson met Fran Walsh. Finding that they shared a dark sense of humor and similar taste in films, the two began a writing partnership that blossomed into a long-term relationship. They have two children together, Kate and Billy, and have cowritten the screenplays for nearly all of Jackson's directorial efforts. Jackson's second film, 1989's *Meet the Feebles,* continued his tendency to push the boundaries of good taste. Richard Corliss of *Time* magazine described it as quite probably "the first all-puppet musical-comedy splatter film," tipping the kid-friendly world of Jim Henson's Muppets on its head. The puppets in *Meet the Feebles* get caught up in drugs, sex, and mass murder. The movie is filled with disgusting displays of bodily functions and fluids. While some moviegoers were no doubt repulsed by the film, others appreciated Jackson's sick sense of humor.

For his next film, Jackson took on a standard of the horror film genre: the zombie movie. In *Braindead,* which was released in the United States in 1992 as *Dead Alive,* a woman is bitten by an infected monkey and turned into a zombie. The film features a growing crowd of the walking dead, destroying a town and attacking citizens. *Brain-*

dead displays extraordinary levels of gore and violence, but the film-maker never takes himself or the film too seriously, injecting heavy doses of campy humor and silliness. The film's hero, for example, tackles a herd of zombies with a lawnmower. *Entertainment Weekly* critic Owen Gleiberman wrote that the film "manages to stay breezy and good-natured even as you're watching heads get snapped off of spurting torsos." Jackson has labeled this blending of comedy and gore "splatstick," a term that can be applied to most of his early films.

In 1994 Jackson directed a film that surprised his hardcore fans. *Heavenly Creatures,* while still displaying a fascination with the darker side of humanity, is a departure in terms of style, avoiding the over-the-top gore of his other films. Depicting the true story of two New Zealander girls, Pauline and Juliet, whose intense friendship and obsession with the fantasy world they create lead them to kill Pauline's mother, *Heavenly Creatures* attracted the notice of critics and film-makers around the world. Jackson's fans knew he was intensely creative and skilled at weaving lighthearted humor into scenes of gruesome violence. But with *Heavenly Creatures,* he revealed an ability to convey subtle and complicated emotions. The story is told from the girls' point of view, and Jackson draws viewers into their world, creating a sense of identification while also confronting the horror of their actions. Cowritten with Walsh, *Heavenly Creatures* received an Academy Award nomination for best screenplay. It lost the award to *Pulp Fiction,* but the film earned such positive attention that it led to greater opportunities for Jackson as a filmmaker.

With *The Frighteners,* Jackson returned to his comedy/horror roots, but this time he had the support of a large Hollywood film studio (Universal), a major star (Michael J. Fox), and a big-name producer (Robert Zemeckis). Determined to stay in his home country, Jackson insisted that the movie be made in New Zealand. His homegrown visual-effects studio, Weta Workshop, created close to six hundred computer-generated special-effects shots for the film. Fox plays a con-man who communicates with the dead and is reluctantly drawn into a hunt for a deadly spirit on a killing spree. Intended as a Halloween release, the film became a victim of schedule juggling and came out in the summer of 1996. It failed to connect on a large scale with audiences, though Jackson's fans happily added it to the list of reasons to marvel at the New Zealander filmmaker.

A gigantic risk

Jackson and Walsh, longtime fans of Tolkien's *Lord of the Rings,* wanted to make a fantasy film and considered the classic trilogy to be the model for all fantasy literature. Wondering why it had not been attempted before, they—and their writing partner Philippa Boyens— began working on a screenplay with the backing of Miramax, the Disney-owned film studio. Problems arose when Miramax became worried about the projected cost, suggesting the trilogy be compressed into one film. Jackson began looking for another studio to finance the film. With a projected cost of nearly $300 million for three films, and with nothing in his past experience to suggest that the New Zealander was the right director for the Tolkien masterpiece, Jackson's pitch was a tough sell. Taking on a great risk, New Line Cinema agreed to back the films, counting on the widespread fan base for the books to bring people into theaters. It was decided that the three films would be shot at the same time, something that had never before been attempted in the history of film. The decision arose from the studio's desire to cut costs, but Jackson came to feel it was the best approach: "I felt that in order to do the tale's epic nature justice, we had to shoot it as one big story because that's what it is," he explained at the *Lord of the Rings* Web site. "It's three movies that will take you through three very unique experiences but it all adds up to one unforgettable story."

Tolkien's novels, first published in the 1950s and read by millions of people in many different languages, transport readers to a distant time in an imagined realm called Middle-earth. An epic battle of good versus evil, *The Lord of the Rings* features a varied collection of creatures, including hobbits, elves, dwarves, and humans, waging war against wickedness. The films boast a huge cast, including Elijah Wood, Viggo Mortensen, Ian McKellan, Liv Tyler, Cate Blanchett, and many others. The actors spent well over a year in New Zealand shooting the film, far away from their homes and families. They learned how to ride horses, sword fight, and speak Elvish, a language invented by Tolkien. Language coaches were brought in to develop a unique accent for a language that had existed only on the page.

Jackson and his crew went to great lengths to create the Middle-earth universe as described by Tolkien, paying attention to every last detail. "From the beginning I didn't want to make your standard fantasy film," Jackson stated in an article at the *Lord of the Rings* Web site.

"I wanted something that felt much, much more real. Tolkien writes in a way that makes everything come alive and we wanted to set that realistic feeling of an ancient world-come-to-life right away with the first film, then continue to build it as the story unravels." In the same article, Blanchett, who plays Galadriel, the elf queen, recalled the vivid world the filmmakers had created: "By the time I started working, there was such a strong and real-life sense of the various cultures, their histories, and their hopes for the future. It was really like becoming part of a whole different universe. I've never experienced anything like it before." The special-effects experts at Weta deserve much of the credit for the films' richly textured universe. The first two installments each have eight hundred special-effects shots, while the third part includes more than fifteen hundred. Such shots are perhaps most crucial to the gigantic battle scenes, which are populated by thousands of computer-generated creatures.

A huge payoff

Jackson understood from the beginning that he had a dual purpose with these films. He felt a tremendous obligation to remain faithful to the books, knowing the intense devotion felt by many Tolkien fans. He also knew, however, that the films had to entertain and make sense to moviegoers who had not read the books. At the film's Web site, Jackson recalled that he, Walsh, and Boyens combed through the books when writing the screenplay; in addition, "every time we shot a scene, I reread that part of the book right before, as did the cast. It was always worth it, always inspiring." The first part, *Lord of the Rings: The Fellowship of the Ring* came out in December of 2001 to great acclaim. Not only were most Tolkien fans impressed by the care Jackson lavished on the film, but millions who had not read the books—and many who had no interest in the fantasy genre—were entranced as well. The film earned more than $850 million at the box office worldwide and garnered numerous award nominations and several victories. *Lord of the Rings: The Two Towers* was released one year later, in December of 2002. Despite the challenges of the second film—which starts abruptly where part one left off and ends without any tidy sense of resolution—*The Two Towers* succeeded phenomenally. Its worldwide earnings exceeded $900 million, and it too received a number of important awards.

Before the release of the third installment, expectations soared. When *Lord of the Rings: The Return of the King* came out in December of 2003, millions of fans breathed a sigh of relief. The conclusion of the trilogy proved as engrossing as the first two segments, and many reviewers wrote of its intense emotional impact. At the film's Web site, Jackson acknowledged the satisfying sense of closure the final film gives: "The journeys these characters have been on, what they care about, what they've been fighting for, what some of their friends have died for, all leads to the events in *The Return of the King*." As many expected, *Return of the King* swept the 2004 Academy Awards, winning the Oscar in every category in which it had been nominated, including best picture, best director, best adapted screenplay, and best visual effects. The film also won best director and other awards at the Golden Globes ceremony and from the British Academy of Film and Television Awards (BAFTA).

Peter Jackson accepts the Best Director Oscar for **The Lord of the Rings: The Return of the King.** AP/Wide World Photos. Reproduced by permission.

In the midst of the release cycle for the three *Lord of the Rings* films, Jackson was often asked by journalists what project he would tackle next. He generally replied that he and Walsh were looking forward to working on another small film on the order of *Heavenly Creatures*. But when the offer came for him to direct a remake of *King Kong,* hardly a "small film," Jackson could not refuse. The original 1933 version was the movie that had made Jackson decide, at the age of nine, to become a filmmaker. He had been offered the chance to direct a *King Kong* remake once before, in the mid-1990s, but funding had fallen through. When the chance came along again, he leaped at it. Having traveled with him to Middle-earth and back, millions of Jackson fans eagerly anticipated the next ride.

For More Information

Periodicals

Corliss, Richard. "Peter Jackson: Lord of the Cinema." *Time* (April 26, 2004): p. 100.

Fleming, Michael. "Oscar Hopeful Serkis 'Towers' over CGI Brethren." *Daily Variety* (November 22, 2002): p. 2.

Flynn, Gillian. "Gory Days." *Entertainment Weekly* (March 22, 2002): p. 63.

Gleiberman, Owen. "*Dead Alive.*" *Entertainment Weekly* (March 5, 1993): p. 40.

McLean, Thomas J. "'King' Maker.' *Daily Variety* (December 19, 2003): p. A6.

Rebello, Stephen. "Peter Jackson's *Bad Taste.*" *Variety* (December 8, 2003): p. S92.

Web Sites

"Andy Serkis: *The Lord of the Rings.*" *Andy Serkis.* http://www.serkis.com/cinlotr.htm (accessed August 1, 2004).

The Lord of the Rings. http://www.lordoftherings.net (accessed August 1, 2004).

"Peter Jackson: The King of the Rings." *BBC News.* http://news.bbc.co.uk/1/hi/entertainment/film/3429373.stm (accessed August 1, 2004).

LeBron James

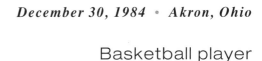

AP/Wide World Photos. Reproduced by permission.

December 30, 1984 • Akron, Ohio

Basketball player

Before LeBron James had completed his sophomore year of high school, basketball scouts were discussing his chances of playing for the National Basketball Association (NBA). Before playing his first regulation game for the NBA, James had signed deals with Nike and other corporations for multimillion-dollar product endorsements. Before he completed his rookie season in the NBA, sportswriters were discussing his chances of joining the most elite players in history in the Basketball Hall of Fame. Comparisons to NBA superstar Michael Jordan (1963–) became common, and some sportswriters began calling James "The Chosen One," indicating the hope that the rookie phenomenon would revive interest in the NBA that had declined since Jordan's retirement. LeBron James, by age eighteen, knew a thing or two about dealing with pressure. James's ability to cope with that pressure has proven to be a critical factor in his success. Sportswriters and his coaches agreed that James has shown uncommon maturity for a player his age, handling his newfound fame and the extraordinary expectations of others with grace.

During 2003, prior to his graduation from high school, James declared himself eligible for the NBA draft, the annual process by which professional basketball teams select new players to join them for the upcoming season. The Cleveland Cavaliers, one of the worst teams in the NBA, had the privilege of the number-one draft pick. The Cavs chose James, with the obvious expectation that this eighteen-year-old would lead the team to greatness. While James's first season with the Cavs did not exactly propel them to a championship, he did help his team win twice the number of games as they had the year before, and at the end of the 2003–04 season, James was named Rookie of the Year.

> **"** I don't want to be a cocky rookie coming in trying to lead right off the bat…. If there's one message I want to get to my teammates it's that I'll be there for them, do whatever they think I need to do. **"**

A team player

Born in Akron, Ohio, in 1984, James is the only child of Gloria James, who gave birth to him when she was just sixteen years old. Gloria struggled to provide for James during his childhood. When James was about five years old, he and his mother moved seven times in a year. For a couple of years during elementary school, James lived with a foster family. Gloria's longtime boyfriend, Eddie Jackson, has acted as a father figure for James, but he was not always around during James's youth, spending several years in prison for selling drugs and, later, for fraud. Regardless of any troubles they may have had, however, James and his mother have a close and supportive relationship. He told Jack McCallum of *Sports Illustrated:* "My mother is my everything. Always has been. Always will be."

Taller and more athletic than most other kids his age, James got hooked on basketball early in childhood. Dru Joyce II, who coached

Another Rising Young Star: Carmelo Anthony

For the 2003 draft, the hype surrounding LeBron James nearly eclipsed another young basketball phenomenon: Carmelo Anthony (1984–). The number-three draft pick with just one year of college basketball under his belt, Anthony would have attracted even more attention than he did, had he not been drafted at the same time as James. His one year of college ball, playing for Syracuse University, had resulted in a National Collegiate Athletic Association (NCAA) championship for Syracuse, with Anthony named Most Outstanding Player of the Final Four, the NCAA championship series.

Anthony was drafted by the Denver Nuggets, a team that joined the Cleveland Cavaliers at the bottom of the NBA rankings. Expectations for Anthony, like those for James, were extremely high: the Nuggets would be relying on him to raise them from the depths and eventually make them playoffs contenders. Anthony performed impressively during his rookie season, racking up an average of 21 points, 6.1 rebounds, and 2.8 assists per game. Perhaps the most significant statistic for his team: the Nuggets went from winning just seventeen games in 2002–03 to winning forty-three games in Anthony's first season.

Anthony grew up in the rough inner city of Baltimore, Maryland. His father died when he was two years old, and his mother, Mary Anthony, raised Carmelo and his three older siblings by herself. She pushed her son to stay focused and disciplined where basketball was concerned, and she pushed him to attend college before going professional. To fulfill his desire to play for Syracuse, Anthony had to leave his Baltimore high school to attend the prestigious Oak Hill Academy, a Baptist boarding school in Virginia. He studied hard to bring his grades up so he could get admitted to Syracuse, and he practiced basketball as often as possible. He helped the Oak Hill team to a number-three national ranking in 2002, and he earned the grades necessary to take him to Syracuse.

Anthony has been described as an unusually mature player who has maintained his down-to-earth style even in the midst of the money, celebrity, and pressure that have come his way. Among the first things he spent his money on after being drafted by the Nuggets were a home for his mother in Baltimore and a youth center there to replace one that was closed down by the police when he was growing up.

James for many of his early years, recalled in an article for the Knight Ridder/Tribune News Service that, while playing in a summer league during elementary school, James was an aggressive offensive player who "really liked to shoot the ball—a lot." Joyce remembered advice he gave James at the time: "I started telling LeBron about passing the ball, how great players make their teammates better. I talked about getting his shots in the flow of the game." Joyce assumed that he would have to repeat this advice many times, reminding the eleven-year-old to be a team player, but he was mistaken. James absorbed every word his coach said and immediately changed his playing style. "That was the last time I ever had to talk about LeBron shooting too much," Joyce recollected.

At the time, James played basketball with his best friends, including Dru Joyce III, the son of his summer-league coach, and Sian Cotton, the son of another summer-league coach, Lee Cotton. Those coaches, both of whom stressed the values of good sportsmanship and being a team player, helped James form the basis of his playing style. James and his pals Joyce III and Cotton, along with Willie McGee, played together every chance they could as kids, and they vowed to stay together all through high school. That childhood promise became a reality as the four boys all attended Akron's St. Vincent–St. Mary High School, a private school known for its basketball program. At St. Vincent–St. Mary, James not only became the school's star basketball player, he also played football for three years and maintained solid grades. James's philosophy about being a team player meant that he spent as much of his playing time passing the ball to teammates and setting up shots as he did taking shots himself, resulting in his extraordinary passing skills. His high school coaches asserted that James could have been a player who averaged fifty to sixty points per game. Instead, his average was closer to thirty points a game, but he helped his entire team play better basketball. Many coaches and sportswriters have described James's maturity and selflessness as a player; Keith Dambrot, who coached James for his first two years of high school, summed up the key to James's success in the Knight Ridder/Tribune News Service article: "LeBron is a basketball genius, there is no other way to say it."

Fast-track to the NBA

Few high school basketball players attract notice outside their home state, but by his junior year, James had caught the attention of basketball fans across the country and earned the intense devotion of fans throughout Ohio. The St. Vincent–St. Mary team won the Division III state championship three of the four years that James attended the school, and in 2002, *USA Today* named the team number one in the country. James was named High School Boys Basketball Player of the Year by *Parade* magazine after both his junior year and his senior year; in forty-seven years of giving out this award, *Parade* has never chosen the same player two years in a row. *Sports Illustrated* put James on the magazine's cover in 2002, only the eighth high school basketball player to be on the cover in forty-eight years. Once word got out about James's extraordinary ability, home games were moved

Lebron James of the Cleveland Cavaliers (left) drives around Shandon Anderson during a 2004 game against the New York Knicks. AP/Wide World Photos. Reproduced by permission.

to a stadium at University of Akron to accommodate the numerous fans who wanted to see him play. Some of those games were even broadcast to national audiences on ESPN and ESPN2. With all that attention came some mild controversy: James received some negative press after his mother obtained a $100,000 loan to buy him a brand-new Hummer H2. He was briefly declared ineligible to play after accepting a gift of two sports jerseys, valued at $845, from a Cleveland store. The abundant attention he had received for his playing, many observers suggested, had made James—nicknamed "King James"—feel that he was entitled to the financial benefits of a seasoned professional. On the court, however, all agreed that James kept his head and continued to play like the member of a team rather than a basketball superstar.

Many observers had wondered, from James's earliest high school years, whether he would go to college or attempt to be drafted into the NBA straight out of high school. Eager to test his skills at the next level, James considered declaring for the draft as a junior, trying to get an exception to the rule that would have barred him from the draft before his graduation year. He decided instead to complete high school, announcing during his senior year that he would declare himself eligible for the 2003 NBA draft. James's decision to go professional right out of high school renewed the debate over whether players should be allowed to play for the NBA at such a young age. Supporters argue that if the player possesses the skills, he should be allowed to earn a living playing his sport. Critics suggest that most high school kids would benefit more from going to college first, using those years to improve their playing, acquire an education, and become more mature. Ignoring the debate and following his own instincts, James opted to skip college and head for the NBA.

Coming off a terrible season, tying for the worst record in the NBA, the Cleveland Cavaliers had a chance to reshape their future in June of 2003: they had the number-one draft pick. They chose James, pinning their hopes on the eighteen-year-old player to turn their fortunes around. At six-foot-eight and 240 pounds, James certainly looked the part of an NBA player. But many wondered if he could live up to the hype surrounding him and compete in the far more competitive arena of professional basketball. When James made his official NBA debut in the fall of 2003 in a game against the Sacramento Kings, he answered the concerns of many doubters. The Cavaliers lost the game, but James played better than most rookies could hope for in a debut game—and better than any rookie straight out of high school—with twenty-five points, nine assists, six rebounds, and four steals. While he occasionally showed his inexperience and youth, and while he did not live up to the most outrageous expectations that he would play like Michael Jordan right out of high school, James did perform extremely well in his rookie season. He ended the 2003–04 season with an average of 20.9 points, 5.5 rebounds, and 5.9 assists per game. He ranked among the top fifteen players in the league in a number of categories, including points per game, total points, assists, and steals. In April of 2004, James was named the

Rookie of the Year for the 2003–04 season. Speaking of the rookie's innate abilities on the court, Cleveland power forward Carlos Boozer told McCallum of *Sports Illustrated,* "You can only call it court sense. The way he takes advantage of a situation right away can't be taught. He just has it."

"I can handle it"

Barring injury, James will earn $19 million for his first four years with the Cavs, an amount that seems downright insignificant when compared to his endorsements. In a sponsorship deal that will pay James more than any other basketball player except Michael Jordan, Nike signed the player to a seven-year, $90 million contract—and that contract was signed before James had even inked a deal with the Cavs. He has also agreed to promote Coca-Cola products, including Sprite and Powerade, and Bubblicious bubblegum.

Predicting the amount of money James will generate for the Cavaliers, for Nike, and even for other NBA teams, *Forbes* magazine suggests that those investing in James will be repaid handsomely. During his rookie season, attendance for Cavs home games increased by fifty percent from the prior season. James sparked so much hype that basketball fans around the country sought out tickets for the Cavs' away games, moving the Cleveland team from last in the league for road attendance to first. As for his corporate sponsors, Nike released the first shoe endorsed by James, the Air Zoom Generation, in December of 2003. At $110 a pair, Nike sold 72,000 pairs in the first month alone. Bob Williams, the CEO of a company that matches athletes with corporations for endorsement deals, described to *Sports Illustrated* in 2003 the hurdles James will encounter in his first few years in the NBA: "He has to dominate his position, take a downtrodden franchise to the playoffs and eventually to a championship. He will make a lot of money and live happily ever after. But no one has ever had more expectations put on him than this young man right now." When reporters have asked him about dealing with the enormous pressure placed on him, James has frequently uttered what has become a sort of motto: "I can handle it." And with one successful season under his belt—both on court and off—many commentators have come to believe that perhaps he can.

For More Information

Books

Jones, Ryan. *King James: Believe the Hype—The LeBron James Story.* New York: St. Martin's Press, 2003.

Morgan Jr., David Lee. *LeBron James: The Rise of a Star.* Cleveland: Gray and Company, 2003.

Periodicals

Badenhausen, Kurt. "Slam Dunk." *Forbes* (February 16, 2004): p. 64.

Chappell, Kevin. "Can LeBron James Repeat the Jordan Miracle?" *Ebony* (January 2004): p. 124.

Finnan, Bob. "Early to Rise." *Sporting News* (October 20, 2003): p. 40.

McCallum, Jack. "You Gotta Carry That Weight." *Sports Illustrated* (October 27, 2003): p. 68.

Pluto, Terry. "LeBron James, Once a Lanky Kid, Has Come a Long Way to the NBA." Knight Ridder/Tribune News Service (April 20, 2004): p. K1569.

Taylor, Phil. "Carmelo Anthony Has a Secret." *Sports Illustrated for Kids* (November 3, 2003): p. 24.

Web Sites

LeBronJames.com. http://www.lebronjames.com/hsc/hscMain.cfm (accessed August 1, 2004).

"LeBron James." *NBA.com.* http://www.nba.com/playerfile/lebron_james/index.html?nav=page (accessed August 1, 2004).

"LeBron Watch." *Cleveland.com.* http://www.cleveland.com/lebron/ (accessed August 1, 2004).

Morgan Jr., David Lee. "The Rise of a Star." *HoopsHype.* http://www.hoopshype.com/articles/lebron_morgan.htm (accessed August 1, 2004).

Steve Jobs

© Kim Kulish/Corbis.

February 24, 1955 • California

CEO of Apple, CEO and chairman of Pixar Animation Studios

Computers had been around long before Steve Jobs entered the field, but his contributions revolutionized the personal-computer industry. As the cofounder of Apple in 1976, Jobs introduced the concept of a small, relatively inexpensive desktop computer that the average person could own and operate. Since that time, Jobs has presided over a number of technological innovations with Apple. He has also made an impact in the field of animated movies as the head of Pixar, the studio responsible for such blockbusters as *Toy Story, Monsters, Inc.,* and *Finding Nemo.* Jobs headed up yet another innovative success story with Apple's online music shop, iTunes, and with its portable digital music player, iPod. Jobs has a reputation for being intimidating to employees and difficult with peers, but he is also seen as a visionary who dreams big and enjoys taking risks. While not all of his risks have paid off, those that have succeeded have significantly altered the high-tech landscape and paved the way for future advances.

Searching for meaning

Steven Paul Jobs was born in California on February 24, 1955. His parents, unmarried and unable to care for a baby, put him up for adoption. He was adopted by Paul and Clara Jobs, who raised him in a northern California community surrounded by apricot orchards and farm country—a community that has since become the center of technological innovation known as Silicon Valley. When Jobs was in the seventh grade, he encountered troubles at school, the victim of bullies. He refused to return to that school, and his parents decided to move to Los Altos. Jobs attended Homestead High School in Cupertino, California, where he had a reputation as a loner and developed a keen

> **"**I think Apple has had a good hand in setting the direction for the whole industry now, again. And that's where we like to be.**"**

interest in technology. During a school field trip to the plant of the Hewlett-Packard computer company in nearby Palo Alto, the concept of a desktop computer attracted Jobs's notice. Later, in pursuit of computer parts for a school project, Jobs went straight to the source, contacting William Hewlett, cofounder of Hewlett-Packard. Jobs got more than just the needed parts; he was also offered a summer job at the company.

During his internship at Hewlett-Packard, Jobs met Steve Wozniak (1950–), an electronics whiz who had attended Homestead High School a few years prior. They formed an immediate bond and soon began collaborating on various projects, including a device that would allow users to make free long-distance phone calls. Wozniak supplied the technological know-how, while Jobs dreamed up ways for consumers to use the products they developed. These roles would remain the same years later, when the two men became reacquainted for a new venture. In the meantime, Jobs graduated from high school in 1972 and then enrolled at Reed College in Portland, Oregon. He dropped out after one semester, but he continued to spend time on

campus, searching for life's meaning: he studied philosophy and meditation, experimented with drugs, and became a vegetarian.

Apple bites back

Jobs returned to California in 1974, restless and looking for work. He answered a help-wanted ad in the newspaper and was hired to work for Atari, a video-game manufacturer that had risen to prominence with Pong, a game that today looks extremely primitive but at the time seemed quite high-tech. According to a profile in *Time* magazine, Jobs's intense personality made him few friends at Atari. "His mind kept going a mile a minute," reported Al Alcorn, the chief engineer at Atari. "The engineers in the lab didn't like him. They thought he was arrogant and brash. Finally, we made an agreement that he come to work late at night." After a short time at Atari, Jobs left to take a trip to India, continuing his quest for spiritual fulfillment. After his return to the

Steve Jobs in 1984. AP/Wide World Photos. Reproduced by permission.

United States, Jobs traveled for a time and then got involved with the Homebrew Computer Club in 1975. At meetings for this club, computer enthusiasts would gather to share information and technology. Jobs's friend from Hewlett-Packard, Steve Wozniak, was a member of the club, and in 1975 Wozniak was still working at Hewlett-Packard and trying to build a computer in his spare time.

Jobs, excited by the prospect of building and selling reasonably priced personal computers, teamed up with Wozniak. While Jobs had a decent grasp on the technology, it was Wozniak who brought the brilliant engineering skills to the partnership. Jobs, on the other hand, was the entrepreneur, the person who understood what they would need to get their business off the ground, how the products would be used, and how to market the products to the public. Jobs and Wozniak formed a company, which Jobs named (he told Jay Cocks of *Time:* "One day I just told everyone that unless they came up with a better name by 5 P.M., we would go with Apple"), and they released their first product, the Apple I, for the price of $666. At that time, few people outside of computer hobbyists felt the need to own a desktop computer, but Jobs

The Man behind the Man: Edwin Catmull

While Edwin Catmull's name may not be as familiar to the average citizen as Steve Jobs's name, his contributions to Pixar have been unparalleled. "Put simply, computer animation and films like *Toy Story* would have never have happened without Ed Catmull," Jobs told Laura Ackley of *Variety.* As president and cofounder of Pixar, Catmull provides exceptional leadership, hiring talented people to work for him and continually striving to keep his employees productive and happy. He has also made tremendous technological contributions to the company, developing new and better ways to create computer-animated films. Catmull has received numerous awards, including three Scientific and Technical Engineering Academy Awards, for his work at Pixar.

Born in 1945, Catmull grew up in Utah. His love for animated movies as a child instilled in him a desire to become an animator, but he felt he lacked the drawing skills and instead studied physics and computer science in college. While pursuing a graduate degree (he has a Ph.D. in computer science), Catmull became interested in the relatively new field of computer graphics, a subject that allowed him to merge his interest in computers with his love for art. He was determined to use this new tool to make movies. During this time, in the early 1970s, Catmull made several technological innovations, including the invention of an animation technique called texture mapping, which allows for a more realistic depiction of an object's texture, whether the object is moving or standing still.

In 1974 Catmull moved to New York to work for Alexander Schure, a wealthy supporter of technological advancements whose passion for making computer-

set out to change that. In 1977 Apple released the Apple II computer, which was a huge success and established the model for personal computers that all other companies attempted to imitate. Three years later, Apple's sales reached $139 million. The company then went public, selling shares to those who wished to invest in Apple.

In 1979 Jobs oversaw the development of a radically new kind of personal computer, one that required little experience with computers and was the first to incorporate a mouse. Called the Lisa (Local Integrated Systems Architecture), the computer sold for $10,000 when released in 1983, a price that put it out of reach for most consumers. The development of the Lisa did lead to Apple's next great innovation, however—a computer that was not only affordable but also easy to use, a critical factor at a time when most people considered computers intimidating and foreign. The Macintosh, released in 1984, brought personal computing to the masses, with its easily understood graphics and point-and-click mouse. Rather than typing in complicated commands, users could simply click on an icon, or picture, on the screen. Jobs's obsession with developing the product, however, had caused

animated movies equaled Catmull's. After several years, Catmull decided to move to California and go to work for the computer-graphics division of Lucasfilm, the company owned by George Lucas, who was then at work creating the first *Star Wars* trilogy. At Lucasfilm, Catmull continued to develop new technology to improve computer animation, and he established his reputation for hiring the right people. In spite of the great strides made by Catmull's division, Lucas decided in 1985 that he wanted to sell that segment of his company, and he instructed Catmull to start looking for a buyer. Catmull approached Steve Jobs, who expressed an interest in the division only as a potentially new computer company, not as a movie studio. Disappointed, Catmull kept looking for a buyer who had the same goal he had: to make the first feature film animated completely on the computer.

One year later, Jobs reconsidered and decided to buy Lucasfilm's computer-graphics division. Jobs named the company Pixar after a device invented by Catmull and George Smith, another computer-graphics pioneer from Lucasfilm; the Pixar made great strides in increasing the speed of the animation process. Jobs appointed Catmull chief technological officer of Pixar, a position he held until 2001, when he was made president. As a top executive at Pixar, Catmull spent several years presiding over the effort to make the company's (and the world's) first feature-length computer-animated movie. That film, *Toy Story,* was released in 1995, and while it boasted great technical achievements, audiences connected with the warm, funny story and fully developed characters. The movie was a huge success, paving the way for Pixar's future efforts, each of which boasted more sophisticated technology than the last—and much of that technological development sprang from the mind of Catmull.

problems at Apple. Many years and much of the company's money had been spent on the product's development, causing many at Apple to wonder whether Jobs had lost sight of the big picture. When Macintosh's initial sales were lower than expected, Jobs was pushed to resign by the company's president and CEO, John Sculley. In 1985 both Jobs and Wozniak left the company they had founded.

To infinity and beyond

While his departing deal with Apple included millions of dollars in severance pay, Jobs, thirty years old at the time, did not consider taking any sort of extended vacation from the high-tech industry. He formed the NeXT Computer Company, releasing his first product in 1988. While the NeXT computer had a number of desirable features—including fast processing speeds and sophisticated graphics and sound—it did not sell well due to its high price and an inability to network with other computers. Jobs then turned his attention to developing new software and improving operating systems, the programs that run all other programs on a computer. During this period, in 1991, Jobs married Laurene Powell; the couple has three children.

In 1986 Jobs bought the computer graphics division of the movie studio Lucasfilm Ltd., which had been formed by George Lucas (1944–), the multitalented filmmaker behind the *Star Wars* movies. With this new company, renamed Pixar Animation Studios, Jobs set out to create a major animated-movie studio. Pixar began by making commercials and short animated films, many of which won prestigious awards. The animation industry quickly understood that this new kid on the block was doing something quite different and doing it exceptionally well. In 1991 Pixar signed a deal with Disney to develop and distribute feature-length animated movies. Four years later Pixar released its debut film, *Toy Story,* the first movie to be completely computer animated. A huge success, *Toy Story* earned more than any other movie that year and came to be one of the most successful animated movies in history. It earned several Golden Globe and Academy Award nominations. At that point, looking to concentrate on Pixar, Jobs sold NeXT to his former company, Apple, for $400 million.

The subsequent Pixar animated movies—*A Bug's Life, Toy Story 2, Monsters, Inc.,* and *Finding Nemo*—continued in the *Toy Story* vein, hitting it big at the box office and earning the adoration of fans. *Toy Story 2* earned the distinction of being the only animated sequel in history to earn more than the original, and it won a Golden Globe Award for Best Picture—Musical or Comedy. Released in 2003, *Finding Nemo* broke box-office records, earned an Academy Award for Best Animated Film, and sold an astonishing eight million copies on the first day of the DVD release.

During 2003, Jobs and Michael Eisner (1942–), CEO of Disney, began negotiating for a new contract between Disney and Pixar. Ten months later, in early 2004, the two companies ended their negotiations without an agreement and announced the upcoming end to their partnership, which would dissolve after the 2004 release of *The Incredibles* and the 2005 release of *Cars.* Jobs had demanded a greater percentage of the films' earnings (under the previous contract, the two companies evenly split the cost of making the films and then divided revenues in half, with Disney getting an additional fee for distributing the movies). Disney refused, and Pixar began its search for a new distribution partner. Taking into account the multibillion-dollar earnings of Pixar's first five films, a number of major studios put in hasty calls to Steve Jobs to talk about a partnership. As Andrew Simons wrote in the *Los Angeles Business Journal,* "Everyone wants to take Steve Jobs to the big dance."

Coming full circle

When Apple began to struggle in the mid-1990s, Jobs agreed to act as a consultant, offering advice on turning the company around. In 1997 he was named Apple's interim CEO—a position intended to be temporary until a permanent CEO was found. Three years later, a permanent CEO was named: Steve Jobs. After returning to the helm at Apple, Jobs made a number of decisive moves that immediately improved the company's fortunes. He simplified the product line, introduced a new version of the Apple operating system, and entered into a cooperative agreement with Microsoft. In 1998 Jobs introduced the iMac. This computer offered sufficiently powerful processors and an affordable price tag, but the key to its success may have been the PC's streamlined design and array of bright colors. Upon Jobs's return to Apple, the company pioneered a wireless technology called Air-Port, which enables users to surf the Internet and print without having anything plugged into their computers. A number of new products followed, some of which, like the iBook and PowerMac, were extremely successful, and some of which were not—including the G4 Cube, which sported a slick design but an out-of-reach price.

Jobs's endless quest for technological innovation soon led him to tackle the digital music industry. In 2001 Apple launched a sleek new handheld product, a portable digital music player called the iPod. Comparable to MP3 players introduced by other companies, the iPod allowed users to download music from CDs or from online sites. Thanks in part to a memorable advertising campaign and good word-of-mouth, Apple sold three million iPods in less than three years. By 2004, almost half of the digital music players bought by consumers were iPods.

Apple's next move, in 2003, was to open an online music store. The music industry had been in a sales slump, with many concerned that such free file-sharing services as Napster, which allowed users to download songs without paying a penny, would spell doom for CD sales. Soon after legal battles complicated the practice of downloading music for free, Jobs opened the iTunes Music Store. Others had attempted online music sales with little success, failing either because they offered a poor selection or because users rejected the notion of paying a monthly subscription fee to download songs. Jobs's iTunes offered simplicity: with the blessing of the world's major record labels, customers could download any of the two hundred thousand songs for just ninety-nine cents each. Users could then create their own CDs with the downloaded songs or transfer them to a portable digital music player, to take with them wherever they go. While iTunes did not live up to Jobs's high expectations of one hundred million downloads in the first year, it did perform astonishingly well. In the first week, one million songs were downloaded, with the total exceeding fifty million after one year. Many observers cautioned that Apple would have to continue to approach online music sales in a creative and aggressive way: while Apple was an early innovator, a number of major players, including Microsoft, Wal-Mart, and some record labels, soon followed suit, offering stiff competition to iTunes.

Many industry observers have noted that, for all its innovation and creativity, Apple has never become a powerhouse in terms of sales. Apple commands just a small percentage of the personal-computer market and earns a tiny fraction of the revenues of its primary software competitor, Microsoft. Jobs shrugs off such details, however, suggesting that it's more important to him to continually create new, original, high-quality products than to become the leader in PC sales. In an interview for *Macworld* on the occasion of the twentieth anniversary of the Macintosh, Jobs summarized his point of view: "Apple's market share is bigger than BMW's or Mercedes's or Porsche's [is] in the automotive market. What's wrong with being BMW or Mercedes?"

For More Information

Periodicals

Ackley, Laura A. "Pixar's Deep Talent Pool Lured by Catmull's Vision." *Variety* (July 20, 1998): p. 32.

Burrows, Peter. "Pixar's Unsung Hero." *Business Week* (June 30, 2003): p. 68.

Burrows, Peter. "Rock On, iPod." *Business Week* (June 7, 2004): p. 130.

Cocks, Jay. "The Updated Book of Jobs." *Time* (January 3, 1983): p. 25.

Hawn, Carleen. "If He's So Smart.… Steve Jobs, Apple, and the Limits of Innovation." *Fast Company* (January 2004): p. 68.

Quittner, Josh. "Steve Jobs: The Fountain of Fresh Ideas." *Time* (April 26, 2004): p. 75.

Simons, Andrew. "Studios Anxiously Jockey to Court Pixar As Jobs Patiently Revels in New Control." *Los Angeles Business Journal* (April 26, 2004): p. 1.

Snell, Jason. "Steve Jobs on the Mac's Twentieth Anniversary." *Macworld* (February 2004).

Web Sites

Apple. http://www.apple.com (accessed August 1, 2004).

Pixar. http://www.pixar.com (accessed August 1, 2004).

Angela Johnson

AP/Wide World Photos. Reproduced by permission.

June 18, 1961 • Tuskegee, Alabama

Writer

Since 1989 Angela Johnson has been steadily producing exceptional books for young people, ranging from picture books for children to novels, poetry, and short stories for young adults. Her works have earned her the adoration of fans and the admiration of reviewers, many of whom have commented on her exceptional ability to create memorable, real characters who stay in readers' minds long after the book cover has been closed. In most of her books Johnson addresses personal, everyday subjects: family relationships, the difficulties of growing up, seeking comfort from loved ones during times of struggle. A number of reviewers have noted that, while many of Johnson's characters are African American, the circumstances they confront and the emotions they express are so true to life that they can be appreciated by all readers. Johnson's editor, Kevin Lewis, stated in an article for the Knight Ridder/Tribune News Service, "A reader might begin thinking that they have nothing in common with [Johnson's characters], but by the end they realize that the list of things people share—things like family, friends, struggle, change, love, loss, dreams, and so on—is much more profound [or, meaningful] than the list of our differences."

The origins of a writer

Born in 1961 in Tuskegee, Alabama, Johnson grew up in Alabama and Ohio. Reading and listening to stories was a significant part of her childhood. Her father and grandfather were natural storytellers, and Johnson can pinpoint the moment when she realized that her own fondness for stories was more than a passing interest. As described on the *African American Literature Book Club (AALBC)* Web site, John-

> **"**Kids and teens are so much more interesting than adults. Life is happening when you are a teenager. One minute you're a child, the next you're allowed to go out in the world by yourself. Who knows what will happen?**"**

son recalled hearing a particularly compelling storyteller during her early school years. She realized that the characters of her favorite books had come alive in her mind, becoming as real as the children sitting next to her in school. "That is when I knew," she remembered. "I asked for a diary that year and have not stopped writing."

One of the ideas that has occupied Johnson as a writer is a child's search for truth or, rather, the quest to uncover what she calls "the big lie"—the feeling that one's parents might not be who they seem, or that the things a child has always accepted as reality might not be true. In an interview in the magazine *Booklist,* Johnson stated: "There's always that point when kids rifle through their parents' papers to make sure they weren't adopted. I was probably about nine or ten when I picked my dad's lockbox with a bobby pin. And it's really interesting because I didn't have that big lie in my life! But I had so many friends

Major Works for Young Adults

Toning the Sweep (novel), Orchard, 1993.

Humming Whispers (novel), Orchard, 1995.

Songs of Faith (novel), Orchard, 1998.

Heaven (novel), Simon & Schuster, 1998.

Gone from Home: Short Takes (short stories), DK Publishing, 1998.

The Other Side: Shorter Poems (poems), Orchard, 1998.

Maniac Monkeys on Magnolia Street (short stories), Random House, 1999.

When Mules Flew on Magnolia Street (short stories), Knopf, 2000.

Running Back to Ludie (poems), Orchard, 2001.

Looking for Red (novel), Simon & Schuster, 2002.

A Cool Moonlight (novel), Dial, 2003.

The First Part Last (novel), Simon & Schuster, 2003.

who did." She went on to say that once she became a writer she realized that "you can get a great story from the big lie."

In the *Booklist* interview Johnson recalled her "fantastic childhood." She acknowledged that she became moody and angry as a teenager, and that during high school her writing was extremely personal. She wrote only for herself, as a way of expressing feelings of frustration and alienation. On the *AALBC* Web site, she described her writing from that period as "punk poetry that went with my razor blade necklace." She recalled in *Booklist,* "I wrote the darkest poetry about cityscapes and disintegration and rats. The literary guild at school wouldn't accept any of my work, which I think nurtured me because it made me even angrier." While she had been writing since early childhood, Johnson was not very interested in reading until a high school English teacher showed her the works of some of the Beat poets, writers who, during the 1950s, wrote experimental, nontraditional verse to challenge mainstream, middle-class ideas about art and life. In addition to such poetry, Johnson enjoyed reading factual works about real people. She explained in *Booklist:* "When I was a teenager, I only read nonfiction. I didn't want to read anything that wasn't true. I was immersed in people's lives—Janis Joplin, Malcolm X. I wanted to know the real story."

Finding her path

After graduating from high school, Johnson attended Kent State University in Ohio, studying special education. She left college without earning a degree, and from 1981 to 1982 she worked in childhood development as a participant in the program known as Volunteers in Service to America, or VISTA. Although she had been writing poetry and stories for many years, Johnson did not think of writing as a realistic career goal. During her college years, though, she met a writer who encouraged Johnson to re-define herself. Working part-time as a babysitter for acclaimed children's author Cynthia Rylant, Johnson was eventually persuaded to show Rylant some of her writing. Recognizing Johnson's gifts, Rylant urged her to focus on writing for young people. A few years later, in 1989, Johnson published her first work, a picture book called *Tell Me a Story, Mama.*

Over the next several years Johnson produced a number of well-received picture books for young children, including *Do Like Kyla, The Leaving Morning, The Girl Who Wore Snakes,* and *Julius.* While she would continue to create picture books for many more years, in 1993 Johnson began to create works with an entirely different focus, releasing her first novel aimed at young adults. *Toning the Sweep* tells the story of fourteen-year-old Emmie, who journeys with her mother to the home of her Grandmama Ola in the California desert. Ola is dying of cancer, and Emmie and her mother have come to help her make the move to Cleveland, Ohio, where she will spend her final months surrounded by family. While in California, Emmie tags along on her grandmother's visits with friends, videotaping their conversations and recording the friends' good-bye messages to Ola. In so doing, she discovers a great deal about her grandmother and about tragic events in her family's past. Reviewers praised Johnson's understated, realistic style of storytelling, noting that rather than spelling out every detail, the author encouraged readers to use their imaginations. In 1994 *Toning the Sweep* won the Coretta Scott King award, an annual honor given by the American Library Association to outstanding works for young people by an African American author.

Johnson's next young-adult novel, *Humming Whispers,* published in 1995, tackled the difficult subject of mental illness. Sophy, fourteen years old and training to be a dancer, worries about her older sister, Nikki, who suffers from schizophrenia, a serious mental disorder that dramatically affects feelings, thoughts, and behavior. Nikki first developed symptoms of her illness at age fourteen, and Sophy's anxieties for her sister also extend to herself: she is concerned that she too will begin to show signs of schizophrenia. Johnson was able to balance the serious and painful subject matter with a strong sense of the strength the characters were able to derive from their family members and friends. A reviewer for *Publisher's Weekly* described *Humming Whispers* as "a story of subtle but real hope, in the form of strong, abiding human connections … and moments of understanding and acceptance."

Family connections also played an important role in Johnson's 1998 novel *Songs of Faith.* Set in a small Ohio town in 1976, this book explores the impact of their parents' divorce on Doreen and her younger brother, Robert. Johnson does not shy away from difficult subjects in her writing, and she portrayed these topics in an honest, realistic light, showing that the love and support of family and friends, while not removing the pain altogether, can help make it bearable.

Johnson has applied her considerable talent for relating memorable characters and interesting situations to other genres as well, including short stories and poems. In 1998 she published *Gone from Home: Short Takes,* a collection of short stories. The following year, she released *The Other Side: Shorter Poems,* a book of verse written in plain, everyday language. The loosely connected poems, based on recollections of her childhood, capture details of life in the small town of Shorter, Alabama. Yet another book, made up of poems that link together to tell a story, *Running Back to Ludie* examines a teenage girl's reunion with the mother from whom she was separated.

Heaven and beyond

In her 1999 novel *Heaven,* another winner of the Coretta Scott King award, Johnson reexamines the meaning of family connections. Fourteen-year-old Marley enjoys a contented, secure life with her parents and brother in a town called Heaven. She goes to school, plays with her friends, and looks forward to the engaging letters she occasionally receives from her traveling uncle. One day she learns that things are not what they seem: her "parents" are actually her aunt and uncle, while her "Uncle Jack" is really her father. Furious that she has been deceived by the people she loves the most, Marley must come to terms with her feelings of anger and betrayal, and she must redefine her notion of family.

In 2003 Johnson set a second novel in the town of Heaven. In *The First Part Last,* she depicts the life of Bobby, a teenage boy who is single-handedly raising his baby daughter. *The First Part Last* is a prequel to *Heaven,* telling a story that takes place before the events that unfold in the 1999 novel. Just sixteen years old, Bobby must abruptly enter adulthood when he takes responsibility for raising his daughter, Feather. The chapters alternate from the past to the present, switching back and forth from the months before his daughter was born to his early struggles as a single father.

Kevin Lewis, Johnson's editor, told the author that a group of sixth graders had said that Bobby was their favorite character from *Heaven.* When he asked her if she thought Bobby could be the subject of a new novel, Johnson initially said no. Johnson recalled in *Booklist,* "At first I thought, absolutely not. Usually, when I finish a book, it's done. The characters have folded up their bags and walked on home." But one day on the subway in New York, she saw a teenage boy with a baby. Her first thought was that the baby was the boy's sister, but then it occurred to her that she could be his daughter. She explained in *U.S. News & World Report,* "I kept thinking about what life would be like for him. Mostly, boys are portrayed as clueless, and they desert their girlfriends. But what about the boy who does the right thing?" From these imaginings, Johnson spun the story of Bobby and Feather, a novel that earned high praise from critics. A *Publisher's Weekly* reviewer wrote: "Each nuanced chapter feels like a poem in its economy and imagery; yet the characters … emerge fully formed." In 2004 *The First Part Last* earned Johnson her third Coretta Scott King award, as well as the Michael L. Printz Award, given for excellence in young adult literature. In early 2004 Johnson announced that she was at work on a third novel set in the town of Heaven.

Recognition beyond expectation

After years of writing books in a variety of forms for a variety of age groups—and earning prestigious awards and high praise from both readers and reviewers—Johnson learned in late 2003 that she was the recipient of an extraordinary honor. She had been named a MacArthur fellow, receiving a $500,000 grant known as the "genius" grant. The prize came from the John D. and Catherine T. MacArthur Foundation, a private organization that, among other things, awards grants to exceptionally talented people in a variety of creative fields. Described by many as humble, shy, and unassuming, Johnson was quite surprised by the news of having won the grant. She explained in *Booklist,* "I'm still shocked—the award is still not real to me. I've been so busy that I haven't actually had time to think about how this will change my life. And I guess it won't. I'll still be the person who wears her PJs all day long." She went on to say that, while the publicity and recognition stemming from the MacArthur grant were exciting, she looked forward to getting back to her normal writing routine. "It may not be mountain climbing, but sitting in front of the computer does it for me. It's easy for me to be thrilled."

For More Information

Periodicals

Corbett, Sue. "'Genius' Label Doesn't Erase Author Angela Johnson's Shyness." Knight Ridder/Tribune News Service (February 25, 2004): p. K4506.

Engberg, Gillian. "The Booklist Interview: Angela Johnson." *Booklist* (February 15, 2004): p. 1074.

"The First Part Last." Publishers Weekly (June 16, 2003): p. 73.

Hallett, Vicky. "When Mr. Mom Is a Teenager." *U.S. News & World Report* (January 26, 2004): p. 16.

"Humming Whispers." Publishers Weekly (January 23, 1995): p. 71.

Web Sites

"Angela Johnson." *African American Literature Book Club.* http://authors.aalbc.com/angela.htm (accessed on March 25, 2004).

"Angela Johnson's Biography." *Visitingauthors.com.* http://www.visitingauthors.com/printable_pages/johnson_angela_print_info.html (accessed on March 25, 2004).

Dwayne "The Rock" Johnson

AP/Wide World Photos. Reproduced by permission.

May 2, 1972 • *Hayward, California*

Professional wrestler, actor

Although Dwayne Johnson is not a superhero out of a comic book, he does have an alter ego. By day he is a somewhat mild-mannered husband and father. But at night when he steps into the ring, he becomes the chair-flinging, wisecracking wrestler known as The Rock. In the late 1990s the charismatic Johnson, with his exotic good looks and signature eyebrow arch, helped make World Wrestling Smackdowns a part of must-see TV. By the mid-2000s, he had such a following that he was dividing his time between the mat and the big screen. Some observers felt that Hollywood had found its next big-budget action idol, and many predicted that Johnson would have no problem filling the shoes of America's favorite muscleman, Arnold Schwarzenegger, who was now busy in his new role as governor of California.

Third generation wrestler

Johnson is a third-generation wrestler. His mother's father, Peter

"High Chief" Maivia, was a professional wrestler of Samoan descent whose heritage served as the basis for his ring persona. Samoa is an island nation located in the South Pacific, and Maivia played the part of an island native, wearing his hair long, wrestling barefoot, and sporting traditional tattoos over most of his body. While on the wrestling circuit he became acquainted with an up-and-coming African American wrestler named Rocky Johnson. During a visit with Maiva's family, Johnson met High Chief's daughter, Ata. The two eventually married, and on May 2, 1972, the couple had a son, whom they named Dwayne Douglas Johnson.

"My work, my goal, my life, it's like a treadmill. And there's no stop- button on my treadmill. Once I get on, I just keep going."

Johnson was born in Hayward, California, but he grew up all over the country, since the family moved around to accommodate Rocky Johnson's wrestling career. Because of the family's frequent moves, young Dwayne had a difficult time making friends. He was also teased by other children about his father's profession, and about his size—even as a youngster, Johnson was bigger than average. As a result, he had a quick temper, and as Johnson admitted to Samantha Miller of *People,* he was even arrested several times for fighting. "It was all youth and stupidity," he explained. In the mid-1980s, however, the Johnsons settled down long enough for Dwayne to begin attending Freedom High School in Bethlehem, Pennsylvania, where an interest in sports helped calm the young man down.

At Freedom High, Johnson boxed and ran track, but he pursued football with a vengeance, hoping to win a scholarship in order to become the first member of his family to go to college. He was a standout star, and by his senior year he was named to *USA Today*'s high school All-American team. Before graduation Johnson was recruited by several colleges, but he chose to head to Florida to attend the University of Miami, where he played defensive tackle. He soon became known for his talents on the gridiron, but was also known for his crazy antics. During one game against San Diego in 1992, millions of people watched on television as he raced around the field chasing the opponent's mascot, a man in a giant Aztec warrior costume.

Johnson's future in football looked bright until he suffered a back injury during his senior year. He was so depressed that he cut classes and his grade point average (GPA) dropped to a dangerously low 0.7. Not only was he sitting on the bench, he was also on academic probation. Johnson pulled himself together, thanks in part to his future wife, Dany Garcia, a business major he met while in Miami. Garcia encouraged him to hit the books, and in 1995 he graduated with a degree in criminology and a respectable 2.9 GPA.

Enter Rocky Maivia

Because of his injury, Johnson was not picked to play for the National Football League (NFL) during the 1995 draft, but he still pinned his hopes on a career in pro football. When he was offered a contract by the Calgary Stampeders, he signed on the dotted line and headed to Canada. Life in Canada was miserable. Johnson saw little field action and was paid less than $200 per week to be a practice-squad player. He rented a tiny, dingy apartment and slept on a mattress he found near a local dumpster. His salary left little room for food, so Johnson took to attending every Stampeder meeting, even though he didn't have to, because he knew sandwiches would be served. He was determined to stick it out, but in an abrupt move, Johnson was let go by the football franchise to make room for a former NFL player. "That was hard," he told Zondra Hughes of *Ebony*. "I was supposed to be reaping the fruits of my labor, and there I was in Canada having to start all over again."

Johnson returned to Florida where both his parents and Dany Garcia lived, and immediately approached his father with a proposal: he wanted to be trained as a wrestler. His decision was made partially out of necessity, but Johnson also had a real love of the sport. After all, he had seen his first wrestling match when he was three weeks old, and when he was six years old his father had taught him such basic moves as the headlock and the armlock. Rocky Johnson, however, had his doubts. He knew that the life of a wrestler was not an easy one and he wanted to spare his son the tough road he had walked.

Rocky finally relented, and for the next few months kept the would-be sparrer on a grueling training schedule.

When he felt prepared enough, Johnson contacted a colleague of his grandfather's, who helped open the door for a tryout with the World Wrestling Federation (WWF) in Corpus Christi, Texas. Although promoters were impressed enough to sign a contract with him, Johnson still had to pay his initial dues by spending some time in Memphis, Tennessee, performing in the WWF second-tier system, the Unites States Wrestling Alliance. During the summer of 1996 Johnson wrestled in promotional matches using the name Flex Kavana, and earned about $40 per night. In August he was given his second professional tryout, this time pitted against a well-known wrestler named Owen Hart. He did so well that he was transferred to Connecticut where the WWF headquarters and training facility were located.

On November 16, 1996, just one year after hitting a low point in Canada, Johnson made his professional wrestling debut at Madison Square Garden in New York City. He performed under the name of Rocky Maivia, a nod to both his father and grandfather. The WWF event was called the Survivor's Series, and Johnson, as Rocky Maivia, was considered to be a "good guy" or, in wrestling terminology, a "babyface." His "bad guy" opponent, or the "heel" in the match, was Paul Levesque, more commonly known as Triple H.

The Rock is unveiled

Johnson quickly became a hit with wrestling crowds, and in February of 1997 he captured his first WWF championship, making him, at age twenty-four, the youngest wrestler to win a belt. But just a few months later Rocky was being booed during matches. Apparently the fickle audience members were becoming much more interested in rooting for the "bad guys," and in a business where image is everything, Johnson had some rethinking to do. In mid-1997, after suffering a knee injury, he took some time off to recuperate, to marry his longtime girlfriend Dany Garcia, and to strategize.

Wrestling in the late 1990s was not the world of wrestling Johnson's father had inhabited. In 1979 the regional federations that existed throughout the United States had been consolidated into a single organization known as the World Wrestling Federation, and by the mid-1980s pro wrestling had evolved from an athletic sport into a form of high-energy entertainment. Wrestlers now admitted that their moves were choreographed and that the outcomes of the matches were pre-determined. Wrestling had become big business, attracting millions of fans and earning millions of dollars for promoters and the main attractions, the wrestlers.

Johnson and WWF writers and producers worked long and hard to come up with just the right image for the handsome, six-foot-four-inch, 270-pound newcomer. What finally emerged was a character named The Rock, who would transform the world of wrestling. According to Johnson, who spoke with Sona Charaipotra of *People,* "The Rock is Dwayne Johnson with the volume turned all the way up." Wearing black boots, black briefs, and with a tattoo of a Brahma bull on his twenty-two-inch bicep, The Rock was touted as part of the Nation of Domination, a league of "bad boy" wrestlers. He also became a formidable force both inside and outside the ring, especially when he glared at opponents and the press with a menacing lift of his right eyebrow.

When The Rock was unveiled on August 11, 1997, in Jackson, Mississippi, the crowd went wild, and over the next several years fans stood in line to catch the next installment in his wrestling storyline. Producers pitted him against various characters in mock grudge matches, and The Rock won, then lost, then regained his federation championship several times. Along the way, Johnson became perhaps the most popular wrestler in the history of the sport. He was known as The People's Champion, and his signature eyebrow move even took on a name—The People's Eyebrow. In addition, The Rock became a merchandising gold mine. His image appeared on T-shirts, posters, and Halloween masks; and there were Rock action figures and video games. By the 2000s, according to Gillian Flynn of *Entertainment Weekly,* the WWF was bringing in $120 million in merchandise sales per year, thanks solely to Johnson.

Pins down the big screen

Johnson's appeal was not limited to wrestling fans, although he is credited with almost doubling the WWF's female fan base, thanks in large part to his movie-star good looks. He was so popular that in 2000, when he published his autobiography, *The Rock Says,* the book stayed on the *New York Times* bestseller list for an astonishing twenty weeks. Johnson drew record crowds at book signings, and began popping up on television, both to promote his book and to take on small acting roles. He made several appearances on the late-night comedy program *Saturday Night Live,* and was featured on such TV shows as *DAG, Star Trek: Voyager,* and *That '70's Show.* The next logical step was the big screen.

In 2001 Johnson appeared briefly in the summer blockbuster *The Mummy Returns,* for which he was paid, in Hollywood terms, a paltry $500,000. Although he was given only minutes of screen time, producers were impressed enough that they built a movie around Johnson's *Mummy* character, called *The Scorpion King.* The film, which was released in 2002, is an action-adventure movie set in ancient Egypt. Johnson plays Mathayus, a desert warrior who is determined to save his people from an evil conqueror named Memnon. If he succeeds, he will take his rightful place as the Scorpion King. Although the movie was definitely not high drama, considering that Johnson's character spent most of his time swinging a sword and slashing his enemies, the would-be actor took his role seriously. In fact, he worked closely with an acting coach throughout the shooting of the film.

When *The Scorpion King* hit theaters in April of 2002, it made more than $36 million during its opening weekend. Critics discussed the digitized action sequences and compared the movie to *The Mummy,* but most focused on Johnson and his million-dollar performance ($5 million, to be exact). In various reviews he was called a big-screen champ and the new face of Hollywood action. As Owen Gleiberman of *Entertainment Weekly* put it, "The Rock commands the screen as naturally as he does the ring."

The Scorpion King opened up a whole new career for Johnson. In 2003 he followed up *Scorpion* with *The Rundown,* another action movie, but one with a comedic edge that allowed him more acting freedom. Again, reviewers were pleasantly surprised. They called *The Rundown* a movie that was a cut above the average shoot-'em-up blockbuster, and they praised Johnson's portrayal of Beck, a bounty hunter set loose in the Amazon jungles of Brazil. In particular, critics praised his comedic abilities, which viewers had glimpsed in his television roles. Johnson's acting coach, Larry Moss, told Gillian Flynn in *Entertainment Weekly,* "The action roles were obviously what he

Sean William Scott (left) and Dwayne "The Rock" Johnson in a still from the movie The Rundown *(2003).* Universal/Columbia/The Kobal Collection/Aronowitz, Myles.

was commercially designed to do in the beginning, but he can play real comedy, and I hope he does after all the action-star stuff."

The most electrifying man in sports

By the mid-2000s, Johnson was a full-fledged movie star. In 2004 he made his dramatic debut in *Walking Tall,* playing Chris Vaughn, a club-wielding sheriff who battles drug dealers and con artists who threaten to take over his peaceful Washington town. There were also several other movies in the pipeline, including two comedies, *Be Cool* (2004), a sequel to the 1995 hit *Get Shorty,* and *Instant Karma,* slated to open in 2005.

Although busy with his many film roles, Johnson still managed to maintain his hectic wrestling schedule. This meant that between filming he was still out on the road, performing and promoting for more than two hundred days a year. Such a demanding schedule was hard on family life, especially considering that Johnson and Dany had their first child, daughter Simone Alexandra, in 2001. Even on the road, however, Johnson claims that he finds the time to call Dany every day, and he still retains close ties to his mother. As Hughes commented, "The Rock is a mama's boy." But The Rock is also a very determined man who has pumped-up plans for the future. As he told Hughes, "I want to do more in the WWF. I want to do more in the movie industry. Ultimately, I want to be the most electrifying man in sports entertainment, period."

For More Information

Books

Johnson, Dwayne, with Joe Layden. *The Rock Says … The Most Electrifying Man in Sports Entertainment.* New York: Regan Books, 2000.

Periodicals

Charaipotra, Sona. "The Rock Sounds Off." *People* (April 19, 2004): p. 30.

Flynn, Gillian. "Rock of Ages: Wrestler, Actor, Action Hero?" *Entertainment Weekly* (May 3, 2002): pp. 10–12.

Gleiberman, Owen. "Rock Formation: The Scorpion King, a Bare-Bones Prequel to the Mummy Movies, Gives The Rock a Solid Step toward Stardom." *Entertainment Weekly* (April 26, 2003): pp. 117–118.

Gostin, Nicki. "Newsmakers: Interview with The Rock." *Newsweek* (April 12, 2004): p. 71.

Hughes, Zondra. "The Rock Talks about Race, Wrestling, and Women." *Ebony* (July 2001): p. 32.

Leyner, Mark. "The Rock is an Onion." *Time* (April 29, 2002): p. 81.

Miller, Samantha. "Bigger, Boulder: Scorpion King's The Rock, a.k.a. Dwayne Johnson, Wrestles with Fatherhood, Fame—and Flab?." *People* (May 6, 2002): pp. 109+.

Web Sites

The Rock Official Web site. http://www.therock.com (accessed on July 6, 2004).

Norah Jones

AP/Wide World Photos. Reproduced by permission.

March 30, 1979 • New York, New York

Singer, songwriter

In 2002 Norah Jones, age twenty-two, released her debut full-length album, *Come Away with Me*. A low-key, acoustic work that defies categorization but includes hints of jazz, traditional pop, country, and folk; the CD is the kind of recording that would ordinarily have sold several thousand copies, earned admiring reviews in the music press, and then faded from view. In the beginning, that is exactly the path the recording seemed to take. But to the surprise of many, including Jones herself, *Come Away with Me* continued to sell steadily month after month, thanks to outstanding reviews, positive word-of-mouth, and unexpected radio play. It took nearly a year, but eventually the album reached the number-one position on *Billboard*'s album chart, selling some three million copies over twelve months. By 2004 it had sold eight million copies in the United States and an additional ten million worldwide. Far less well known than her fellow nominees, Jones earned five nominations for Grammy Awards. On February 23, 2003, the night of the 45th Annual Grammy Awards, she went home with an armload of tro-

u·x·l newsmakers • volume 2

phies, winning for every category in which she was nominated. Her follow-up album, *Feels Like Home,* followed a different, steeper path when released in 2004: Jones's second effort shot straight to number one, selling one million copies in its first week alone.

From NYC to Grapevine and back to NYC

Jones was born in New York City in 1979. Her mother, Sue Jones, is a nurse and music promoter. Her father, Ravi Shankar, is a world-famous musician hailing from India. Shankar became widely known for his association with the Beatles and other Western musicians; he

> "I'm not soft-spoken and romantic, at all. I must be, somewhere deep down, otherwise I wouldn't like that kind of music. But I'm only like that when I'm on stage. I'm pretty much just loudmouthed, obnoxious, and silly."

taught Beatles' guitarist George Harrison how to play the sitar, a long-necked Indian stringed instrument, of which Shankar is considered a master. As early as age three, Jones began showing a keen interest in music, closely watching her father when he played his sitar. At age five she began singing in her church choir. She learned to play several instruments in her youth, primarily studying piano. Shankar and Sue Jones, unmarried when Norah was born, separated when she was still a young child. Sue took her daughter to live in Texas in a suburb of Dallas called Grapevine. Jones lived there for much of her childhood, having no contact with her famous father for ten years. Her musical influences during that time came from her mother's record collection. She felt especially affected by the works of great jazz, soul, and blues singers, including Etta James, Aretha Franklin, and Billie Holiday. Jones also spent countless hours listening to recordings of musicals such as *Cats* and *West Side Story.*

Brit Crooner Jamie Cullum

Norah Jones's surprising success with a style of music that generally doesn't reach the top of the *Billboard* charts has paved the way for similar artists, performers who now see the potential for widespread success with their more traditional musical styles, and whose labels are now more willing to invest in their music. One such performer, Britain's Jamie Cullum, has crafted a jazz-influenced style for his singing and piano playing, a blend of old-time pop standards and cabaret-style jazz with the occasional rock tune thrown in for good measure. With *Twentysomething,* Cullum has taken his native country by storm, selling more records than any other jazz artist in United Kingdom history, and outselling a number of major pop acts as well. He made a splash in the United States when his album was released there in 2004, with many critics comparing his swinging style to that of Norah Jones and Harry Connick Jr., and to the croonings of another famous performer, the late Frank Sinatra.

Just twenty-three years old at the time of his 2003 U.K. release of *Twentysomething,* Cullum took his newfound fame in stride, considering it the result of many years of working hard and paying dues. He has been playing guitar and piano since age eight, and he began playing for audiences in clubs and bars at about age fifteen. Encouraged in his love of jazz by his older brother, Ben, Cullum grew up admiring jazz greats Oscar Peterson and Dave Brubeck. In an inter-

view with *WWD* magazine, he related that he was also heavily influenced by other types of music: "I grew up listening to Public Enemy and Kurt Cobain and the Beastie Boys and Guns N' Roses. That's really the influence that pervades what I do." He studied film and English literature at Reading University in England, releasing his first album, as the Jamie Cullum Trio, at age nineteen. His second release, *Pointless Nostalgic,* earned considerable airplay on British radio and earned him a dedicated fan base. The success of that album sparked a bidding war among record labels, with Universal Records winning out. Still in his early twenties, Cullum was signed to a multi-album deal worth over one million dollars.

Cullum has attracted attention for more than just his recorded music: his live performances indicate a young man with over-the-top showmanship. He does more than just play the piano: he bangs on it with his fists, pounds the keys, and occasionally kicks the keys for additional emphasis. When asked by *WWD* about his exuberant style, Cullum replied: "It's a very spontaneous thing. I just let myself go at the expense of looking like an idiot all the time and getting really hot and sweaty and not being very classy." While some reviewers have criticized Cullum for lacking subtlety, others have praised his boundless energy onstage and applauded his efforts to bring lighthearted fun to music that is usually played with a more serious tone.

During her high school years at Dallas's Booker T. Washington School for the Performing and Visual Arts, Jones explored her developing passion for jazz. On her sixteenth birthday she gave her first solo performance, singing and playing piano at a coffeehouse on open-mic night, when anyone brave enough can try his or her hand at performing for the public. During that period Jones also played in a band called Laszlo and tried her hand at composing jazz tunes. She earned recognition from the highly respected jazz magazine *Down Beat,* winning their Student Music Award (SMA) for Best Jazz Vocalist two years running and also winning an SMA for Best Original Composition. After graduating from high school Jones enrolled at the University of North Texas. She spent two years there, studying jazz piano and giving solo performances at a local restaurant on weekends. She also became reacquainted with her father, and the two developed a close relationship. The summer after her sophomore year Jones decided to head to New York City and try her luck making it as a musician there.

Pounding the pavement

Working in a restaurant during the day and performing in downtown clubs by night, Jones felt excited to be part of the city's jazz scene, rather than just studying music in a classroom. She decided to stay in New York, forming a jazz trio, and also performing with other jazz groups, including the Peter Malick Group. While her professional life revolved mainly around jazz, she began listening often to country music. She told *Texas Monthly,* "It's funny, but I got into country music when I moved to New York. I was homesick, so I listened to [renowned country singer-songwriter] Townes Van Zandt." She created a demo recording of her solo work to send to record labels in the hope of getting a deal, but after a year of passing her demo around with no success, she began to feel discouraged.

On the evening of her twenty-first birthday, Jones gave a performance that connected deeply with a notable member of her audience. Shell White, an employee in the accounting department of the revered jazz label Blue Note, was so struck by Jones's talents that she arranged for a meeting between the young singer and the label's chief executive officer (CEO), Bruce Lundvall. After meeting Jones and hearing her sing, Lundvall signed her to a record deal on the spot. Lundvall explained to *Time* magazine's Josh Tyrangiel that such impulsive decisions had been made only twice in his career at Blue Note (the other artist was jazz vocalist Rachelle Ferrell). Lundvall described the essence of Jones's appeal: "Norah doesn't have one of those over-the-top instruments. It's just a signature voice, right from the heart to you. When you're lucky enough to hear that, you don't hesitate. You sign it."

"Snorah" Jones makes good

Jones began her relationship with Blue Note by releasing a six-song EP, a less-than-full-length recording, called *First Sessions*. This CD includes several songs that later showed up on *Come Away with Me*. For her debut full-length recording, Blue Note paired Jones with veteran producer Arif Mardin, who had worked with such legendary performers as Aretha Franklin and Dusty Springfield. When she and Mardin began recording *Come Away with Me* in May of 2001, Jones showed a preference for a spontaneous style in the studio, aiming to capture the intimate and natural qualities of live performance. She recorded fourteen songs for her debut; Jones wrote a few of the tracks but left most of the composing duties to others, including her boyfriend, bassist Lee Alexander, and New York–based songwriter-guitarist Jesse Harris. She also recorded two songs made famous by musicians legendary in their respective fields: country king Hank Williams ("Cold, Cold Heart") and revered jazz-pop composer Hoagy Carmichael ("The Nearness of You").

Released in early 2002, *Come Away with Me* earned positive reviews. Music critics expressed appreciation for her distinctive voice and authentic, understated style. Many critics wrote of Jones as a promising new artist, a refreshing change of pace from the slick packaging of pop stars like Britney Spears. Even the most admiring reviewers, however, did not predict that the album would gradually become a smash hit and that Jones would become Blue Note's best-selling artist ever. *Come Away with Me* became so successful that it seemed to be everywhere: on the radio, on television, playing over the public address system in shopping malls. Jones recalled to Tyrangiel that she heard one of the album's tracks in an unexpected place: "Once on a plane—you know how they play elevator music before you take off?—they played one of the songs." The album's exposure became so great that a small backlash arose, with some music journalists declaring that the attention was nothing but hype, and criticizing Jones's music as bland and boring. Some even started calling her "Snorah Jones," a nickname Jones found amusing rather than hurtful. She confided to Tyrangiel, "My mom calls me Snorah all the time now."

The "insanity," as Jones frequently characterized the buzz surrounding her debut, seemed to reach a peak when the album was nominated for eight Grammy Awards. Competing against such high-profile artists as Bruce Springsteen and Eminem, Jones swept the awards cere-

Norah Jones holds her five Grammy Awards. AP/Wide World Photos. Reproduced by permission.

mony in February of 2003. The album won all eight awards for which it was nominated, with Jones receiving five awards and the three others going to producer Mardin, the album's engineers, and songwriter Jesse Harris for "Don't Know Why." Among Jones's victories were trophies for Album of the Year and Best New Artist. As the ceremony progressed, Jones began to feel overwhelmed, as she related in *Texas Monthly:* "I felt like I was in high school and all the popular kids were in the audience and were, like, 'What's she doing up there?' I felt like I had gone in a birthday party and eaten all the cake before anyone else got a piece." Some aspects of her newfound fame pleased her, especially the positive reception from most critics and her increased ability to control the direction of her career. But for the most part Jones retreated from the spotlight. She preferred the idea of being a member of a group rather than a solo star, telling *Billboard*'s Melinda Newman, "Deep down, in my gut, all I want to be is part of a band." In the beginning, she didn't feel entirely comfortable performing in concert, making music videos, or talking to the press. Jones sought a quiet lifestyle, unexpected for such a young musician, preferring low-key get-togethers with her bandmates to late-night partying at clubs.

A homey follow-up

When work began on a follow-up album, *Feels Like Home,* many music-industry insiders speculated that it would take a miracle for the second album to sell as well as the first. Such predictions did not faze Jones. Her primary focus was the music; she was eager to branch out on her second album and explore different styles, having shifted away from jazz and toward country in her listening habits and writing. For *Feels Like Home,* Jones took a greater role in the songs' composition, writing or cowriting six of the album's thirteen tracks. The album was recorded after a series of collaborative sessions with bandmates, with each member contributing to various aspects of the project. Guest artists included country-music mainstay Dolly Parton and, from the influential rock group the Band, Levon Helm and Garth Hudson.

After the phenomenal success of her debut, people throughout the industry—record label executives, music retailers, and journalists—as well as millions of fans eagerly anticipated Jones's follow-up. Released in early 2004, *Feels Like Home* was snapped up by one million buyers in its first week, resulting in an instant rise to the number-one position on *Billboard*'s album chart. Determined to let her second album's reception happen somewhat naturally, Jones pressured Blue Note to devise an understated publicity campaign that wouldn't blanket the television and radio airwaves with commercials for *Feels Like Home.* Blue Note CEO Lundvall told *Billboard*'s Newman, "We're not hyping the record. We're not going out there and advertising all over the world." For her part, Jones remained calm under the intense pressure of following up a debut album that had sold more than eighteen million copies worldwide. She related in *Texas Monthly:* "It's funny, but I don't want to know about sales. I don't want to read any of the reviews; I don't want to see any of the articles. I just want to do what I do and have it be as unfussed-with as possible."

Music reviewers varied in their responses to *Feels Like Home.* Some expressed a wish that Jones would break out of her mellow approach and make edgier music. David Browne of *Entertainment Weekly* concluded that "Jones' voice conveys warmth and content-ment but little in the way of urgency or intensity." Others felt that she had failed to commit to a specific style, instead sampling from a vari-ety of genres. A few complained that Jones had written or chosen too many mediocre songs, relying on her lush vocals to overcome any writing shortcomings. But numerous critics found plenty to love in Jones's second release. Tom Moon wrote in *RollingStone.com,* "Far from blanded-out background music, *Feels Like Home* … is a triumph of the low-key, at once easygoing and poignant." Matt Collar wrote for *All Music Guide* that, with *Feels Like Home,* "You've got an album so blessed with superb songwriting that Jones' vocals almost push the line into too much of a good thing." At the *PopMatters* web site, Ari Levenfeld wrote: "While many critics of the album complain about the slow pace of the music, relegating it to little more than back-ground music, it's hard to believe that they were paying attention. There simply isn't another singer working in pop music now that holds a candle to Jones."

Millions of fans seemed to agree with Levenfeld's assessment, finding Jones to be a breath of fresh air in a stale pop landscape. She is a musician who has sought success but not necessarily stardom, and who seems more likely to share the spotlight than grab it for herself. At a time when young pop singers belt out every note with over-the-top passion, Jones opts for subtlety, understanding that a low-key voice stripped to its essence can pack a greater punch than one bel-lowed out at top volume. Tyrangiel explained, "She never fails to choose simple over flamboyant, never holds a note too long. She may prove to be the most natural singer of her generation."

For More Information

Periodicals

Browne, David. "Falling in Lull Again." *Entertainment Weekly* (February 13, 2004): p. 70.

Burwell, Alison. "The Jazz Singer." *WWD* (May 11, 2004): p. 4.

Jones, Norah. "No Fuss." *Texas Monthly* (April 2004): p. 60.

Moon, Tom. "As 2nd CD Is Released, Norah Jones Fights for Control of Her Image." Knight Ridder/Tribune News Service (February 11, 2004): p. K4996.

Newman, Melinda. "Norah Jones." *Billboard* (January 31, 2004): p. 1.

Patterson, Troy. "No Place Like Home." *Entertainment Weekly* (February 20, 2004): p. 34.

Tyrangiel, Josh. "Come Away Again." *Time* (February 9, 2004): p. 64.

Tyrangiel, Josh. "Jazzed about Ms. Jones." *Time* (March 18, 2002): p. 84.

Willman, Chris. "Norah Jones." *Entertainment Weekly* (December 20, 2002): p. 36.

Web Sites

"The Complete Norah Jones." *RollingStone.com.* http://www.rollingstone. com/?searchtype=RSArtist&query=norah%20jones (accessed on June 21, 2004).

Levenfeld, Ari. "Norah Jones Hangs Her Hat." *PopMatters.* http://www.pop matters.com/music/reviews/j/jonesnorah-feelslike.shtml (accessed on June 21, 2004).

"Norah Jones." *All Music Guide.* http://www.allmusic.com (accessed on June 21, 2004).

Dean Kamen

AP/Wide World Photos. Reproduced by permission.

1951 • Long Island, New York

Inventor, entrepreneur

Dean Kamen is a leading American scientist and inventor whose products include the Segway human transporter (HT) and the iBOT battery-powered wheelchair. His numerous inventions include medical devices and futuristic gizmos that Kamen hopes will revolutionize the way we live and travel. Whenever Kamen introduces a new product, people take notice, and they eagerly anticipate the next one. His newest creation? A nonpolluting, low-power water-purifying system designed for use in underdeveloped countries. *Time* magazine called it one of the "coolest inventions of 2003."

A modern-day Edison

Dean Kamen was born in 1951, in Rockville Center, Long Island, New York. His father, Jack, was an illustrator for *Weird Science* and *Mad* comic books; his mother, Evelyn, was a teacher. Kamen began tinkering with gadgets when he was fairly young. He claims that when he was five years old he invented a way to make his bed without running from one side to the other.

However, despite the fact that he was obviously bright and very curious, Kamen did not do well in school. His grades in junior high and high school were only average, and Kamen often found himself at odds with his teachers. This is an experience that many creative people seem to go through. For example, Thomas Edison (1847–1931), who developed the electric light bulb and the phonograph, attended school for a grand total of three months. His teachers considered him to be a slow learner. Instead Edison was taught by his mother at home, where he thrived, reading every book he could get his hands on. Like Edison, Kamen was (and still is) an avid reader of science texts.

"If you start to do things you've never done before, you're probably going to fail at least some of the time. And I say that's OK."

By the time he was a teenager, Kamen was being paid for his inventions, most of which he built in his parents' basement. He was hired by local rock bands and museums to design and install light and sound systems. He was even asked to work on automating the giant ball that is lowered in Times Square each year on New Year's Eve. Before he graduated from high school, Kamen was earning about $60,000 a year, which was more than the salaries of both his parents combined.

After high school Kamen attended Worcester Polytechnic Institute (WPI) in Massachusetts, but again he was more interested in inventing than attending classes. It was during his early years at WPI that Kamen developed the first of his many medical breakthroughs. His older brother, Barton, who was in medical school, commented to him that patients who needed round-the-clock medication were forced to come into the hospital for treatment. Kamen decided to fix the problem. He came up with the AutoSyringe, a portable device that could be worn by patients and that administered doses of medication. As a result, patients were able to enjoy some freedom.

A Look at FIRST

Dean Kamen established FIRST (For Inspiration and Recognition of Science and Technology) in 1989 because he wanted kids to get excited about science. A science competition seemed like a good idea, but he did not have a run-of-the-mill science fair in mind. Instead, Kamen developed a robotics competition. The first robotics competition took place in a small New Hampshire high school gym and involved only twenty-eight teams. In 2004 there were more than eight hundred teams in the United States and around the world, competing in twenty-three regional events and a championship event held in Atlanta, Georgia. But, what is a robotics competition all about?

It is a lot like a high school athletic event where teams compete in games of skill, except in robotics, the game changes every year. In early January, FIRST releases the rules of the game, which include how the playing field will be set up and what tasks a robot will be expected to perform to win the most points. For example, in 2004 a robot had to collect balls and deliver them to a human player who shot the balls into a goal.

Teams are then given six weeks to design, build, and test their robots. Companies sponsor local high school teams, providing money to help with costs and technical support to help build the actual robot. The company engineers also serve as mentors to the students throughout the experience.

At regional competitions the atmosphere is charged. Teams wear colorful T-shirts and uniforms that they design with their logo; they also cheer and root for their favorite players. Music is played over loudspeakers, and announcers and referees broadcast during the matches. Teamwork is encouraged. As part of the game, teams are paired together during each match. In match thirteen, Team 182 may be *partnered* with Team 115; in Team 182's next match they be *competing* against Team 115.

Winners at the regional level move on to the national competition in Atlanta, where ultimately one winning alliance (composed of three teams) takes the title. On the FIRST Web site, however, Kamen explains that winning is not what matters: "Here, whether your robot wins or not, you come away … with an understanding of what is possible in the world.

In 1976 Kamen left Worcester Polytechnic (without graduating) and founded his own company, called AutoSyringe, to sell his medication device. The medical community embraced the AutoSyringe, and among scientists Kamen soon gained a reputation as a maverick inventor. In 1982 Kamen sold AutoSyringe to Baxter International, an international health-care company. The sale made him a multimillionaire.

Kamen wows the world

After selling AutoSyringe, Kamen moved to Manchester, New Hampshire, where he launched his new company, DEKA Research & Development. DEKA is a combination of the first two letters of

Kamen's first and last names: DEan KAmen. The DEKA research facility is a vast network of nineteenth-century brick buildings that sprawl along the banks of the Merrimack River. Over two hundred researchers, engineers, and machinists work there and focus both on developing products for other companies and advancing Kamen's own projects. For example, in 1993 Kamen and company invented a portable kidney dialysis machine called HomeChoice. A kidney dialysis machine is used to purify the blood of someone whose kidneys do not function properly. Usually a patient must go to the hospital on a regular basis to be treated.

Kamen went on to impress the medical world by developing hundreds of inventions. In 1999, however, he wowed the rest of the world when he unveiled the Independence iBOT 3000 Mobility System, a stair-climbing wheelchair. "I just thought the existing wheelchair was a pretty inadequate solution," Kamen explained to Max Alexander in a *Smithsonian* interview. The iBOT is a motorized wheelchair that can take on almost any terrain, for example sand, gravel, or grass. It can also climb stairs and curbs, and it raises itself up, balancing on two wheels, so that a user can be level with a standing person. According to Kamen, the stair-climbing capability was great, but for years wheelchair-users had told him they longed to be able to carry on a conversation eye-to-eye.

In 2003 the iBOT was finally approved for sale by the U.S. Food and Drug Administration (FDA). The FDA is a government agency that researches products to make sure they are safe for people to use. The iBOT went into production in late 2003 and was available at a cost of $29,000. People who bought an iBOT were required to go through special training on how to use the system.

The super scooter

If the iBOT caused a media flurry, then Kamen's next invention, the Segway, created a media blizzard. Kamen had been working on his mystery project for over ten years, and months before it was launched there was a buzz about what it could possibly be. In December 2001, Kamen finally introduced the world to what he called a self-balancing, electric-powered transportation machine. Some observers claimed it looked like a super scooter. In a 2001 interview with John

Dean Kamen rides his invention, the Segway Human Transporter. AP/Wide World Photos. Reproduced by permission.

Heilemann, however, Kamen claimed that the Segway would "be to the car what the car was to the horse and buggy."

The Segway has no brakes, no engine (it is battery-powered, so it needs to be charged), and no steering wheel. It can carry a rider who weighs up to 250 pounds, and cargo up to 75 pounds. And it can travel at speeds up to 17 miles an hour. The amazing thing about the machine is that, like the iBOT, it is totally self-balancing, which means it cannot tip over when a person is riding it. Both inventions rely on a system of gyroscopes, computer chips, and electronic sensors that together pick up tiny shifts in the rider's movements. Basically, the Segway does what you want it to do. For example, if you step off, the Segway comes to a stop.

Kamen had high hopes for the Segway. He did not see the Segway as a toy scooter; he believed that it could help solve the problem of overpopulated cities. "Cities need cars like fish need bicycles," Kamen told Heilemann. The inventor envisioned people in cramped urban areas, like San Francisco, California, or Shanghai, China, scooting around on their Segways. As a result, pollution and congested city traffic would be eliminated. Kamen also predicted that the Segway would be used by postal workers, police officers, factory workers, and even soldiers on battlefields.

By 2004 the Segway was not quite as successful as Kamen predicted: only six thousand machines had been sold. Buyers were curious, but not curious enough to pay $4,950 to own one, and problems were cropping up everywhere. The company had to recall, or take back, models because riders were falling off their Segways when the machines' batteries went low. In addition, laws in several cities, including San Francisco, prevented people from riding Segways on city sidewalks. A major blow came in February of 2004 when Segways were banned from Disney-owned theme parks. It seemed that people were not quite ready for the ride of the future.

A global challenge

In 2003 Kamen was ready to tackle another serious problem: contaminated water. During the 1990s he had experimented with a way to power the iBOT and the Segway. He focused on the Stirling engine, which was developed in 1816 by Scottish inventor Robert Stirling (1790–1878), because it produced efficient power that was clean and quiet. It was also complicated and expensive to build. The Stirling engine was not right for his transportation machines, but Kamen believed he could use it to help make clean water. According to the United Nations, an organization of countries working together to keep peace and solve problems, approximately six thousand people die every day from drinking water that is not clean or safe.

After the media hype that surrounded the Segway, Kamen was cautious about predicting the success of his water purifier, nicknamed the Slingshot. It was still costly to produce, but it was small, weighing about one hundred pounds, and it could run on almost any fuel, including wood, grass, or cow dung. Plus, the purifier required little maintenance and would make ten gallons of drinking water an hour. In November of 2003, Kamen told Lev Grossman of *Time* magazine that he was not sure how to market the Slingshot or how to get it to the people of the world who needed it; what he did know was that it works. In 2004 a determined Kamen visited the African countries of Rwanda and Bangladesh to demonstrate his system. He planned to visit India and Pakistan later in the year.

The pied-piper of technology

Throughout his career Dean Kamen has received an amazing number of awards, including the Heinz Award (1998), "for a set of inventions that have advanced medical care worldwide," and the National Medal of Technology (2000). Kamen's National Medal acknowledges his inventions, but it also applauds him for "innovative and imaginative leadership in awakening America to the excitement of science and technology."

Kamen's passion for science has created a need in him to ignite that spark in others, especially young people. According to Max Alexander, he is a "one-man band banging the cymbals of scientific innovation." In 1989 he founded FIRST (For Inspiration and Recognition of Science and Technology). The focus of FIRST is an annual competition where high school teams, with the help of corporate sponsors, build robots and face off in regional and national games. The goal of FIRST is to get young people excited about technology. As a result, they might even consider a career in math, science, or engineering to be an appealing option in a society that idolizes actors, rock bands, and sports stars. Kamen told *Forbes's* Glenn Rifkin, "We'll be successful when you can walk up to the average kid on the street and he'll be able to name a few heroes who … don't dribble a basketball."

One of those heroes just might be Kamen. Since he unveiled the Segway on national television, Kamen has become something of a celebrity. He is an easily recognizable figure, with his shock of dark hair and his trademark uniform of jeans, denim shirt, and work boots. Kamen is also a savvy salesman who tirelessly crows about his inventions. Such salesmanship has made Kamen a very rich man. He lives in an enormous house in Manchester, Connecticut, that is powered by a giant wind turbine and has a fully equipped machine shop in the basement. Out back there is a lighted baseball diamond and a landing pad for his two helicopters, which Kamen helped design. He also owns an island off the coast of Connecticut.

And there is no sign that Kamen is slowing down. Unmarried and with no children, his work seems to be his life, but, as he comments on the Segway Web site, "You know, it's only work if you'd rather be doing something else."

For More Information

Periodicals

Alexander, Max. "'Wow, Isn't That Cool!'" *Smithsonian* (September 2003): p. 95.

Grossman, Lev. "Water Purifier: Thousands Die Every Day for Lack of Clean Water. Can the Man Who Invented the Segway Save Them?" *Time* (November 17, 2003): p. 72.

Heilemann, John. "Reinventing the Wheel: Here 'It' Is.' *Time* (December 10, 2001): pp. 70–76.

Levy, Steven. "Great Minds, Great Ideas." *Newsweek* (May 27, 2002): p. 56.

Rifkin, Glenn. "Geek Chic: Dean Kamen Hopes to Encourage Students to Study Sciences and Technology." *Forbes* (February 26, 1996): pp. S40–43.

Web Sites

For Inspiration and Recognition of Science and Technology (FIRST) Web site. http://www.usfirst.org (accessed on May 29, 2004).

Science Enrichment Encounters (SEE) Science Center Web site. http://www.see-sciencecenter.org (accessed on May 30, 2004).

Segway Web site. http://www.segway.com (accessed on May 30, 2004).

Beyoncé Knowles

AP/Wide World Photos. Reproduced by permission.

September 4, 1981 • Houston, Texas

Singer/actress

From her early childhood, Beyoncé Knowles wanted to be more than a performer: she wanted to be a superstar. By the age of twenty-one, she had reached that goal, becoming world-famous not just in her chosen field of singing but also as an actress. After attaining wide success with the R&B group Destiny's Child, Knowles broke out on her own, releasing her solo debut, *Dangerously in Love,* in 2003. The single "Crazy in Love," featuring her boyfriend, rapper Jay-Z, was one of the biggest hits of the summer of 2003. The song propelled the album to multimillion-unit sales and earned Knowles a number of awards, including a Grammy Award and an MTV Video Music Award. In 2002 she displayed her acting abilities in the third installment of Mike Myers's Austin Powers series *Austin Powers in Goldmember,* starring as Foxxy Cleopatra. The following year she appeared opposite Academy Award–winning actor Cuba Gooding Jr. in *The Fighting Temptations.* Knowles also nabbed a number of high-profile endorsement deals, acting as a spokesperson for Pepsi and for the cosmetics company L'Oréal. For all her money, fame, and critical recognition, Knowles has managed, according to friends, family, and even journalists, to hold on to her warm, genuine nature.

The search for stardom

Beyoncé Giselle Knowles was born and raised in Houston, Texas, along with her younger sister, Solange, who would later follow her sister into the entertainment industry. Her father, Mathew, worked for many years as a sales representative selling medical equipment, while her mother, Tina, worked in a bank and later opened her own beauty salon, which

> "My main accomplishment is achieving peace and happiness. Sometimes you think it's success, and you think that it's being a big star. But I want respect, and I want friendship and love and laughter, and I want to grow."

became one of the most successful salons in Houston. As a young child, Knowles was shy and had few friends. Her parents signed her up for a dance class when she was seven years old, "to make friends more than anything else," as Tina Knowles described to *Essence*. The first time Beyoncé's parents saw her perform, they were stunned. "When we saw her on stage for the first time, it was incredible. I'd never seen her so alive and confident," Tina recalled. Beyoncé had found a way to break out of her shyness, and along the way she discovered she had real talent. She began singing in—and winning—local talent contests, and soon her parents realized that performing made their daughter happy, and that she was gifted enough to have a shot at success.

In 1990, at the age of nine, Knowles auditioned for a singing group called Girl's Tyme. She won a spot with the group and began performing with them at local events. Knowles's cousin, Kelly Row-

Solange Knowles: Joining the Family Business

Talent runs in the Knowles family. Right on the heels of Beyoncé is her little sister, Solange, who, like her more famous sibling, has wanted to be an entertainer for as long as she can remember. She started her life as a professional performer at age thirteen when she began touring with Destiny's Child as a backup dancer. She broke into the music business soon after, releasing her first album, *Solo Star,* in early 2003. Solange has also participated in the theater since early childhood, acting in a number of plays. She made her big-screen debut in 2004's *Johnson Family Vacation,* appearing with Cedric the Entertainer, Vanessa Williams, and rapper Bow Wow.

Solange was born on June 24, 1986, in Houston, Texas. She performed in a children's dance troupe at the age of four and can clearly remember loving the attention and admiration she got from the audience. She was hooked, and knew from that moment on that she wanted to entertain people. She began writing songs since the age of seven, and at age thirteen she asked her parents to allow her to pursue a professional singing career. They suggested she wait until she was a little older. That same year, when one of the backup dancers for Destiny's Child had to drop out just before the start of a tour, Solange

was chosen to fill in. She embarked on a two-year worldwide tour, accompanied by her father, the manager of the group, and her mother, the group's stylist. Her parents watched her closely, observing how Solange handled the hard work and pressures of being on tour. By its conclusion, they had decided their younger daughter was mature enough to begin her own singing career.

Solange knew her way around a recording studio, having spent time with her sister when Destiny's Child was recording. She had learned how to write and produce songs, and she put those skills to use in crafting her debut album, *Solo Star.* With songwriting and production help from such notable artists as the Neptunes, Timbaland, and big sister Beyoncé, Solange created a pop R&B album that showed the influence of reggae, hip-hop, and even country. The album features guest appearances from Da Brat, Lil' Romeo, and B2K.

In early 2004 Solange, at age seventeen, took a break from her career path to wed Daniel Smith, a college football player from Houston. With the rest of the Knowles family looking on, the couple were married in the Bahamas.

land, was also a member of Girl's Tyme, and when Rowland and her mother encountered financial problems, the Knowles family took Kelly in. The members of Girl's Tyme felt that success was close by when they participated in the television talent competition *Star Search* in 1992, but they did not win the contest. Believing that he could improve their chances of getting a record deal, Mathew Knowles became the group's manager and persuaded the group not to give up on their dream. Eventually he quit his job to manage the group full-time, taking them to talent competitions in Los Angeles, California, and elsewhere. He poured his energy, his time, and the family's money into the project, forcing the family to sell their house and move into an apartment. The stress of their reduced circumstances caused problems in Tina and Mathew's marriage. "I felt like the group was more important to him than his family," Tina told *Essence*. The couple separated for a short period, but soon realized they were miserable when apart. They reunited and have been together ever since.

Felt like Destiny

The girls' group, performing under such names as Somethin' Fresh, the Dolls, and Destiny, completed a demo recording to send to record labels. They performed wherever they could, practiced singing and dancing all the time, and, particularly for Knowles and one other girl in the group, they endured strict diets to keep their weight down. The joy they felt when they were signed to a deal in 1995 with Silent Partner Productions, a division of Elektra Records, turned to bitter disappointment when the deal fell through. In 1997, however, Columbia Records signed the group, which had settled on the name Destiny's Child. They started by recording "Killing Time," a song that appeared on the soundtrack for the blockbuster hit *Men in Black.* Soon they began working on their first album. In 1998 Destiny's Child—consisting of Knowles, Rowland, LaToya Luckett, and LaTavia Roberson—released their self-titled debut. Their first single, "No No No," found a huge audience, quickly selling over one million copies and reaching the top of the R&B charts. While not a smash hit, the album performed well overall, selling enough to encourage the girls to return to the studio to record a second album.

After the release of the first Destiny's Child album, the group was one among many all-female R&B groups jockeying for success, but with *The Writing's on the Wall,* released in 1999, they shot to superstardom. The first track, "Bills, Bills, Bills," hit number one on the R&B chart and on the pop charts as well. A subsequent song, "Say My Name," performed even better, and in 2000 Destiny's Child won two Grammy Awards. Their newfound success, however, was not enough to keep the group together. Problems concerning money and decision-making powers drove them apart, and Roberson and Luckett left Destiny's Child. They later sued the group and manager Mathew Knowles, a move that created a stir in the media. The new Destiny's

Child, now including Farrah Franklin and Michelle Williams, felt frustrated that so many media reports focused on the band's troubles rather than their music. In the end, however, the wave of publicity generated by the controversy resulted in more album sales for the group, and *The Writing's on the Wall* eventually sold more than eight million copies.

Franklin quit Destiny's Child after only a few months, leaving the group a trio. One of the problems voiced by departing members was what they considered Mathew Knowles's unfair emphasis on his daughter's career rather than that of the whole group. Whether because of her father or because of her own talent and ambition, Beyoncé had emerged as the group's most visible member. For the third album, *Survivor,* she took an expanded role in the writing and producing, and her increased involvement paid off. When the album came out in the spring of 2001, it shot straight to number one on the *Billboard* 200 album chart, spawning two hit singles with the title track and with "Bootylicious," and winning another Grammy Award. Destiny's Child soon announced that each member would pursue solo projects, although the group, which had sold more than thirty-three million records worldwide, voiced no plans to separate permanently.

Beyoncé Knowles performs at the 2003 Nelson Mandela AIDS Benefit Concert in South Africa. AP/Wide World Photos. Reproduced by permission.

Spreading out

In addition to beginning work on a solo album, Knowles began pursuing acting jobs. In 2001 she appeared as the title character in an MTV production called *Carmen: The Hip-Hopera,* a modern retelling of the nineteenth-century opera *Carmen* by Georges Bizet. Her next acting job exposed her to millions of filmgoers all over the world. Playing the sassy 1970s-era character Foxxy Cleopatra, Knowles helped Mike Myers capture the bad guys in *Austin Powers in Goldmember* in 2002. She then obtained a more substantial role in *The Fighting Temptations,* released in 2003. While the film did not achieve blockbuster status, it did earn more than $30 million at the box office, thanks in large part to Knowles's massive fan base. Aware of the mixed track record of other pop stars crossing over to film, Knowles took her acting seriously, working hard to improve her skills and sincerely hoping to turn in a quality performance. In an article in *People,* Jonathan Lynn, director of *The Fighting Temptations,* recalled of Knowles: "On the first day of filming she was a little nervous. She was aware that I might be treating her with kid gloves, so she took me aside and said, 'Make sure you're happy with what you get from me.'"

Also in 2003, Knowles released her debut solo recording, *Dangerously in Love.* With a list of impressive collaborators including Jay-Z, Missy Elliott, Sean Paul, and Big Boi of the hip-hop duo Out-Kast, Knowles used the album to display a side of herself not previously seen by Destiny's Child fans—more mature, more adventurous, and with songs like "Naughty Girl" and "Baby Boy," more sensual. The breakout single, "Crazy in Love," peppered the airwaves, becoming a huge summer hit in 2003. Featuring the rapping of Jay-Z and describing the giddy feeling of falling hard for someone, the song fueled speculation that Knowles and Jay-Z were romantically linked, but the pair kept the relationship under wraps, determined to keep their personal lives private. *Entertainment Weekly*'s Nancy Miller praised Knowles for exploring a variety of styles on her solo outing, opting to take chances rather than simply continue in the Destiny's Child mode. "While living *Dangerously in Love,*" Miller reported, "[Knowles] birthed contagious hip-hop dance tracks, '70s-R&B-flavored jams, and garment-rending ballads."

The album, released in June of 2003, sold close to three million copies in the United States in its first six months. Knowles was a smash hit overseas as well, with both the "Crazy in Love" single and the album reaching the top of *Billboard*'s European sales charts. Knowles earned a slew of awards after the release of *Dangerously in Love,* taking home five Grammy Awards in 2004, including Best Contemporary R&B Album. Her five statues put her in fine company: only Lauryn Hill, Alicia Keys, and Norah Jones had won that many Grammy Awards in a single year. During 2004 the National Association for the Advancement of Colored People (NAACP) nominated Knowles for five Image Awards, giving her their Entertainer of the Year honor. Knowles's accomplishments have been considerable, but so are her expectations. In an interview with *CosmoGirl!* she explained that her ultimate goal is to be thought of as a legend. In response to the question of what makes a celebrity into a legend, Knowles told *CosmoGirl!*: "When you say her name, what you think about is her star quality. She is a good person, has good spirit, and is more than just a person who performs and sells records. She's a person who will change your life." Knowles may be too young to be described as a legend, but she has joined the elite ranks of Madonna, Cher, and other single-named stars, becoming known to millions of fans simply as "Beyoncé."

For More Information

Periodicals

Chocano, Carina. "Destiny Awaits." *Entertainment Weekly* (May 30, 2003): p. 34.

Feiwell, Jill. "Working on a Dual Destiny." *Daily Variety* (March 5, 2004): p. A8.

Mayo, Kierna. "Beyoncé Unwrapped." *Essence* (August 2003): p. 122.

Miller, Nancy. "Beyoncé: Love Child." *Entertainment Weekly* (December 26, 2003): p. 32.

Rosenberg, Carissa. "Above and Beyoncé." *CosmoGirl!* (September 2002): p. 139.

Sexton, Paul. "Charts Show Europe's 'in Love' with Beyoncé." *Billboard Bulletin* (July 25, 2003): p. 1.

Tauber, Michelle. "Destiny's Woman." *People* (October 6, 2003): p. 87.

Web Sites

"About Solange." *Solange.* http://www.solangemusic.com/ (accessed June 26, 2004).

"Beyoncé." *All Music Guide.* http://www.allmusic.com (accessed on June 24, 2004).

"Biography." *Beyoncé.* http://www.beyonceonline.com/ (accessed on June 25, 2004).

Daniel Libeskind

May 12, 1946 • *Lodz, Poland*

Architect

AP/Wide World Photos. Reproduced by permission.

From a very young age, Daniel Libeskind (pronounced LEE-buh-skinned) exhibited a sharp intellect and extraordinary talents. As a child in Poland, he discovered that he had considerable musical talents; he appeared on live Polish television at the age of six, playing the accordion. As a young man, having immigrated to the United States during his teen years, Libeskind abandoned his musical ambitions, devoting himself to a different type of creative expression: architecture. After studying to become an architect, he spent many years teaching and developing his theories of design rather than actually creating buildings. By the start of the twenty-first century, with one building to his credit—the Jewish Museum Berlin—Libeskind had proven that he could translate his teachings and ideas into a work of tremendous significance, and he came to be considered one of the world's most innovative architects.

A Childhood Propelled by Music

Libeskind was born in Lodz, Poland, on May 12, 1946, the year after World War II (1939–45) ended. Libeskind's parents, Jews living under the dangerous regime of Nazi Germany, had separately fled Poland when the war began. After reaching the border of the Soviet Union, both were arrested by the Soviets. They met and married in 1943, while in exile from their native Poland. After the war, they returned to Libeskind's father's hometown, Lodz, to find that nearly every relative, eighty-five people in all, had been killed during the Holocaust, Nazi Germany's systematic attempt to destroy the entire Jewish population of Europe. Like many Jews in postwar Eastern Europe, the

> **"**I arrived by ship to New York as a teenager, an immigrant, and like millions of others before me, my first sight was the Statue of Liberty and the amazing skyline of Manhattan. I have never forgotten that sight or what it stands for.**"**

Libeskinds found that the formal end of the Holocaust did not bring an end to violent anti-Semitism, or hatred of Jews, in their city. Libeskind told Stanley Meisler of the *Smithsonian:* "Anti-Semitism is the only memory I still have of Poland. In school. On the streets. It wasn't what most people think happened after the war was over. It was horrible." His parents wanted him to play an instrument, but moving a piano through the courtyard of their apartment complex would have aroused the hostility and resentment of the neighbors. Instead, Libeskind's parents bought him an accordion, an instrument that could be concealed in a briefcase. He excelled in his musical studies and earned some measure of fame at a very early age.

When Libeskind was eleven, he, his parents, and his older sister immigrated to Tel Aviv, Israel. Upon moving to Israel, he switched instruments and began playing piano. Two years later, in 1959, he won

Buildings by Daniel Libeskind

The following list indicates the architectural projects, both completed and ongoing, of Daniel Libeskind. The building name is followed by Libeskind's name for or description of the project, the location of the building, and the years of development; the projects are listed in chronological order.

Jewish Museum Berlin, "Between the Lines," Berlin, Germany, 1989–1999.

Felix Nussbaum Haus, "Museum ohne Ausgang," Osnabrëck, Germany, 1995–1999.

Danish Jewish Museum, "Mitzvah," Copenhagen, Denmark, 1996–2003.

Extension to the Victoria & Albert Museum, "The Spiral," London, England, 1996–2006.

Imperial War Museum North, "Earth Time," Manchester, England, 1997–2002.

Studio Weil, Private gallery for Barbara Weil, Port d'Andratx, Mallorca, Spain, 1998–2003.

Jewish Museum San Francisco, "L'Chai'm: To Life," San Francisco, CA, 1998–2005.

Maurice Wohl Convention Centre, Bar-Ilan, "The Book and the Wall," Bar-Ilan University, Tel Aviv, Israel, 2000–2004.

Extension to the Denver Art Museum, "The Eye and the Wing," Denver, CO, 2000–2005.

London Metropolitan University Post-Graduate Centre, "Orion," London, England, 2001–2003.

World Trade Center Site Plan, "Memory Foundations," New York, NY, 2002–.

an America-Israel Cultural Foundation scholarship, which enabled the family to move to the United States. They settled in a one-bedroom apartment in the Bronx, a borough of New York City. Libeskind continued to study music and to perform, but as he matured, he found music to be less and less satisfying. He told Paul Goldberger of the *New Yorker,* "Music was not about abstract, intellectual thought—it was about playing. I didn't find it interesting enough. I couldn't see spending my life on a stage." Craving a different kind of creative and intellectual exploration, Libeskind enrolled in the Bronx High School of Science.

Transition to Architecture

Not long after completing high school, in 1965, Libeskind became a naturalized American citizen. That same year, he chose to study architecture, enrolling at the Cooper Union for the Advancement of Science and Art. Libeskind told Cathleen McGuigan of *Newsweek* that his pursuit of architecture seemed like a natural progression, as it is a field that "combines so many of my interests. Mathematics, painting, arts. It's about people, space, music." When the World Trade Center was under construction, Libeskind used to wander down to the site, as he related to Devin Leonard of *Fortune* magazine: "We used to come down here at lunch when the trade center was being built. It was the most incredible building in New York."

During his college years, Libeskind married Nina Lewis, who would later become his business partner as well, running nearly every aspect of his firm as it grew in size and importance over the years. The couple would go on to have three children: Lev, Noam, and Rachel. After graduating from Cooper Union in 1970, Libeskind studied the history and theory of architecture at Essex University in Colchester, England, earning a master's degree there in the early 1970s.

After completing his education, he briefly held jobs with standard architectural firms, but he felt stifled by what he viewed as a conformist attitude in such offices. He did not want to imitate other people's design ideas and architectural theories; he wanted instead to develop his own notions and encourage other young architects to think independently as well. He decided to pursue teaching. He taught at the University of Kentucky, and at universities in Toronto, Canada, and London, England, before accepting the job, at age thirty-two, as director of the prestigious Cranbrook Academy of Art in Bloomfield Hills, Michigan, a suburb of Detroit. In 1985, after seven years as director of Cranbrook, Libeskind moved to Milan, Italy, to found his own small school, Architecture Intermundium. According to Libeskind, as quoted by Stanley Meisler of the *Smithsonian,* he wanted the school to offer "an alternative to traditional school or to the traditional way to work in an office.... The school was between two worlds, neither the world of practice nor of academia." Libeskind was the only professor at his school, teaching about a dozen students at a time.

The Jewish Museum Berlin

By the end of the 1980s, Libeskind had been teaching architecture for close to twenty years but had yet to actually create the design for a building. His ideas, and his reputation as a thinker and teacher, however, were sufficient to win him an invitation for the competition to design

"Reflecting Absence": The World Trade Center Memorial

In the nights following the September 11, 2001, attacks on the World Trade Center, architect Michael Arad, a New York resident who grew up in Israel, the United States, and Mexico, found himself walking the streets of the city, unable to sleep. He was surprised and moved to find impromptu memorials springing up all over the downtown area, evidence of New Yorkers' intense feelings of grief and loss. Within a few months, he had begun thinking of a way to design a public memorial to honor those who died in the attacks. His initial idea involved creating voids, empty spaces, in the Hudson River near the World Trade Center site. When he heard the announcement that a competition would be held to choose the designer for the World Trade Center memorial, Arad decided to enter.

Well over five thousand people submitted entries for the competition. The jury, including noted architect Maya Lin (1959–), designer of the Vietnam Veterans Memorial in Washington, D.C., narrowed the entrants down to eight finalists. In January 2004, Arad's design was selected. Suddenly, the thirty-four-year-old architect was faced with a tremendous task. He was responsible for what could arguably be described as the most delicate aspect of the complicated World Trade Center redevelopment. His memorial, a highly public place that would be visited by millions every year, would also have to convey a sense of quiet intimacy for the many thousands of people who lost loved ones in the attacks.

Arad's design involves converting the footprints, or foundations, of the destroyed twin towers into thirty-foot-deep reflecting pools. From ground level, the pools will appear as empty spaces, signifying the loss and absence of those who died there. Visitors will be able to descend to the underground memorial, where the names of those who died will be randomly arranged around the reflecting pools; the names of rescue workers will be highlighted with a special symbol. Beneath the reflecting pools, an interpretive center will be built that will house exhibitions and artifacts of 9/11, including personal belongings recovered from Ground Zero and crushed steel beams. The memorial will also include a private room where relatives of the victims can go to pay their respects.

Upon leaving the underground memorial, visitors will enter a large public plaza. Initially Arad had designed this plaza to be fairly bare, and his design struck many as being too severe. After being selected as a finalist in the memorial design competition, Arad joined with California-based landscape architect Peter Walker (1932–) to refine his design. Among other changes, Walker greatly increased the number of trees and other vegetation that would fill the memorial plaza, the area surrounding the memorial. The park-like space will be filled with a variety of deciduous trees and other plants, reminders of the continuation of life in the midst of tragedy, as well as numerous park benches that will allow for rest and contemplation.

the Jewish Museum in Berlin, Germany's capital city. Libeskind won the competition, and in 1989 he began work on the museum, a project that would take a decade to complete. While the museum would present the entirety of Jewish history in Berlin, Libeskind believed that the Holocaust, a defining event for Germany and particularly for German

Jews, would have to be significantly represented. At the Daniel Libe-skind Web site, the architect explains that he realized "the necessity to integrate physically and spiritually the meaning of the Holocaust into the consciousness and memory of the city of Berlin." Having lost so many relatives to the Holocaust, Libeskind felt a special connection to the project. The form the building takes—a long, angular zigzag—represents a sort of flattened, rearranged version of the six-pointed Jewish Star, or Star of David, which millions of Jews in Germany, Poland, and elsewhere were forced by the Nazis to wear on their clothing as a means of identification. The shape of the building was also derived from the locations of the homes of some important Berlin Jews. Libeskind plotted out these addresses, drew lines connecting them, and used the resulting shape as inspiration for the building's design.

Libeskind encountered numerous delays in the planning and construction of the building, which was finally completed in 1999,

The Jewish Museum in Berlin, Germany, designed by Daniel Libeskind. AP/Wide World Photos. Reproduced by permission.

only to stand empty for two years as various decision-making groups in Berlin argued over the exact purpose of the museum. During that period, more than three hundred thousand people came simply to walk through the empty building, drawn to Libeskind's startling, unusual design. On September 9, 2001, the museum, now filled with exhibits, opened to the public, becoming one of Germany's most-visited museums by the end of 2002.

Made of reinforced concrete and covered in zinc, the Jewish Museum Berlin boasts many unique features. Libeskind conceived of an area known as the Voids, empty rooms that run the length of the building, separate from the exhibition halls. According to the Jewish Museum Berlin Web site, "The line of Voids, a series of empty rooms … expresses the emptiness remaining in Europe after the banishment and murder of its Jews during World War II. The Voids stand for the deported and exiled masses, and for the generations that were never born. They make their absence visible."

The museum also includes the Garden of Exile and Emigration, commemorating the hundreds of thousands of Jews who were forced out of Germany during the Nazi reign and acknowledging those who were able to make new lives in Israel. The garden contains forty-eight pillars filled with soil from Berlin; the number recalls the year, 1948, in which the state of Israel was established. A forty-ninth pillar contains soil from Jerusalem, the capital of Israel. Planted in each pillar are olive branches, a symbol of peace. Another part of the museum is the Holocaust Tower, an area found at the end of a hallway. After visitors enter the tower, a heavy gate clicks shut behind them, emphasizing the sense of finality and loss evoked by the Holocaust exhibits. The walls are bare concrete and the space is not heated, reminding visitors of the raw, inhumane conditions of the Nazi prison camps in which millions of Jews died.

McGuigan of *Newsweek* described the Jewish Museum Berlin as "a slash, a wound in the cityscape—a zinc-covered zigzag, its windows diagonal slits. Inside, the spaces are haunting and disorienting." The museum drew international attention and acclaim to Libeskind, and he came to be counted among the most interesting and important architects in the world. In the *Smithsonian,* Meisler explained that "Libeskind is usually described in architectural books as a 'deconstructivist'—an architect who takes the basic rectangle of a building, breaks it up on the drawing board and then reassembles the pieces in a much different way." Meisler noted that Libeskind himself does not consider himself a deconstructivist; he points out his emphasis on "preconstruction as well as construction." In other words, Meisler wrote, "Libeskind collects ideas about the social and historical context of a project, mixes in his own thoughts, and transforms it all into a physical structure." His ability to create a building that has a practical purpose as well as a deep symbolic meaning contributed to the recognition he received for his innovative design of the Jewish Museum Berlin and also played an important role in future commissions.

Triumph and Trouble at Ground Zero

After completing the Jewish Museum Berlin, Libeskind received important commissions to design buildings all over the world, including the Imperial War Museum North in Manchester, England; an extension, known as the Spiral, to the Victoria & Albert Museum in London, England; the Danish Jewish Museum in Copenhagen, Denmark; and the Felix Nussbaum Haus, a museum devoted to a Jewish artist killed during the Holocaust, in Osnabrück, Germany. However, the accomplishment that brought Libeskind to the attention of millions in the United States and elsewhere was his victory in the contest to become the master site planner of the new development at the World Trade Center site, known as Ground Zero, in New York City. Competing against many of the world's most accomplished architects, Libeskind conceived a design that incorporated, in its every aspect, the significance of the tragedy that took place at that site on September 11, 2001, when terrorists crashed two jetliners into the twin towers of the World Trade Center. "But," he explained to Richard Lacayo of *Time* magazine, "we also want to reassert [the area's] vitality." While the jury that had been formed to award the commission did not actually vote in favor of Libeskind, choosing instead the team known as Think, led by Rafael Vinoly and Frederic Schwartz, Governor Pataki (1945–) and other important players, including the families of victims of the attacks, felt a strong connection to Libeskind's design, and he was declared the winner in February 2003.

Libeskind's plan, titled *Memory Foundations,* included a number of features, all interconnected and serving to express his vision of the site as a tribute to the victims of 9/11 and as a landmark architectural project for

New York and the entire United States. His original design designated large areas of open space, including the Park of Heroes as a tribute to those police, fire fighters, and rescue workers who lost their lives on 9/11. Another open space was called the Wedge of Light, a triangular area that, every September 11, would be bathed in natural light, unobscured by shadows from the surrounding buildings, between 8:46 A.M., when the first plane struck one of the twin towers, and 10:28 A.M., when the second tower collapsed. Libeskind's design specified that the seventy-foot-deep "footprints," or foundations, of the collapsed towers—where hundreds worked for many months after September 11, 2001, removing debris and searching for remains—would be left intact as sunken memorial space. Libeskind also wanted to leave standing the slurry walls, which made up part of the foundation of the twin towers, the only part of those buildings to survive the collapse. At the Web site of the Lower Manhattan Development Corporation, the organization that sponsored the search for the site plan designer, Libeskind is quoted as saying, "The foundations withstood the unimaginable trauma of the destruction and stand as eloquent as the Constitution itself, asserting the durability of Democracy and the value of individual life." His concept included a series of buildings to hold offices, residences, a performing arts center, and shopping centers; the tallest building was to be 1,776 feet, a number chosen by Libeskind to recall the year the United States gained independence from Britain. The shape of the building, which was to be topped by a tall spire, would echo that of the nearby Statue of Liberty.

Upon winning the commission, Libeskind—the architect at that point of a handful of buildings, not one of which was a skyscraper—was faced with the enormous task of overseeing the design of a sixteen-acre parcel of land. These were no ordinary sixteen acres, however. Any major development in a large urban area like New York City presents a challenging array of obstacles for an architect, including political concerns, financial needs, the complications of working in a crowded city, and the wishes of the city's residents. The World Trade Center development added a new dimension to this complexity: for the families of the victims of 9/11, and for many others as well, the ground at this site is sacred, and the process for developing that land is charged with strong opinions and deeply felt emotions.

When he was announced as the new developer of the master site plan, Libeskind was abruptly thrust into the limelight. The press fol-

Daniel Libeskind (center) stands behind the model for his design to replace the World Trade Center. AP/Wide World Photos. Reproduced by permission.

lowed his every move, photographers snapped his picture, and his name appeared in the headlines of every major newspaper. Once the excitement died down, Libeskind was forced to confront the complexity of his role. He had to please a number of different factions, or groups, including the Port Authority of New York and New Jersey, the transit management group that owns the land; developer Larry Silverstein, who holds the lease on the property and who would be the recipient of the insurance payout from the twin towers' collapse; Governor Pataki and New York City mayor Michael R. Bloomberg (1942–), both of whom considered the development of the site as a key part of their political legacies; the Lower Manhattan Development Corporation, the government agency that had been created to oversee the rebuilding of Ground Zero; and the families of the victims.

Libeskind found that, in addition to pleasing many different parties, he would also have to cooperate with other architects on the design of the entire complex. He had been chosen to develop the master plan for the site, but he had not been charged with actually designing the different parts of that plan. Silverstein had previously hired architect David Childs (1941–) to design the tallest tower of the site, which has been dubbed the Freedom Tower. Regardless of the fact that Libeskind had submitted his own design for the tower as part of his overall plan for the site, he was forced to collaborate with Childs on a design that would result in both men compromising their initial visions. The memorial at the site would also be handed over to a different architect. An international contest was held to determine the designer of the memorial, and Michael Arad (1969–), a thirty-four-year-old architect, was chosen in early 2004.

Within a year of winning the opportunity to oversee the new World Trade Center complex, Libeskind's original plan had undergone dramatic changes. His tall tower had been changed completely by Childs; his suggestions for memorial space had been overridden by the design of Arad; plans for the slurry walls to remain standing had been scrapped due to engineering concerns; and his proposal for the Wedge of Light plaza had been incorporated as an element of Spanish-born architect Santiago Calatrava's design for the new transportation station.

While the reality of the World Trade Center commission turned out to be far more complex and tangled than Libeskind may have bargained for, and while he surely will have to compromise far more than he would like, the project still offers him the opportunity to be at the helm of one of the most significant building projects in American history. The new World Trade Center could benefit greatly from Libeskind's unique ability to take lofty ideas and powerful emotions and translate them into the physical forms of buildings.

For More Information

Periodicals

Cockfield, Errol A., Jr. "Arad's Vision Reshapes Lower Manhattan." *Newsday* (February 23, 2004).

Eylon, Lili. "Libeskind Zigzag in Berlin." *Architecture Week* (November 7, 2001).

Goldberger, Paul. "Urban Warriors." *New Yorker* (September 15, 2003): p. 73.

"An Interview with WTC Memorial Designer Michael Arad." *Architectural Record* (March 2, 2004).

Lacayo, Richard. "O Brave New World!" *Time* (March 10, 2003): p. 58.

Leonard, Devin. "Tower Struggle." *Fortune* (January 26, 2004): p. 76.

McGuigan, Cathleen. "Daniel Libeskind Takes Home the Prize." *Newsweek* (March 10, 2003): pp. 58–60.

Meisler, Stanley. "Daniel Libeskind: Architect at Ground Zero." *Smithsonian* (March 2003): p. 76.

Novitski, B. J. "Libeskind Scheme Chosen for WTC." *Architecture Week* (March 5, 2003).

Web Sites

Daniel Libeskind. http://daniel-libeskind.com/daniel/index.html (accessed on May 30, 2004).

Jewish Museum Berlin. http://www.jmberlin.de/ (accessed on May 30, 2004).

"Memorial Design." *Lower Manhattan Development Corporation.* http://www.lowermanhattan.info/rebuild/memorial_design/default.asp (accessed on May 30, 2004).

"Studio Daniel Libeskind." *Lower Manhattan Development Corporation.* http://www.lowermanhattan.info/rebuild/new_design_plans/firm_d/default.asp (accessed on May 30, 2004).

Lindsay Lohan

AP/Wide World Photos. Reproduced by permission.

July 2, 1986 • *New York, New York*

Actress

Lindsay Lohan was introduced to filmgoers in 1998 when she faced the difficult task of filling the shoes of beloved child actress Hayley Mills in a remake of *The Parent Trap*. Lohan offered herself up for comparison again five years later when she starred in *Freaky Friday,* another classic teen film from a generation ago. Remakes can be tricky, having to live up to the expectations of fans of the original while also appealing to those seeing the film for the first time. In both of these films, Lohan offered a fresh perspective on her characters while staying true to the spirit of the originals, earning the admiration of a broad spectrum of viewers and the adoration of her teenage and preteen fans. Lohan was crowned one of the new teen queens, with her freckled face suddenly appearing on magazine covers everywhere. She hosted *Saturday Night Live* in May of 2004 and the MTV Movie Awards the following month. More than just a pretty face, Lohan had become an in-demand actress, appearing in two 2004 films, *Confes-*

sions of a Teenage Drama Queen and *Mean Girls,* with plans to star in no fewer than four films in 2005.

A childhood spent in front of cameras

Born on July 2, 1986, Lindsay Morgan Lohan was a member of a family with close connections to show business. Her father, Michael, a former child actor, has dabbled in a number of careers; he owned a pasta business, worked in finance as a Wall Street trader, and produced films. Lohan's mother, Dina, has also proven to be multitalented. The former professional dancer, one of the world-famous Radio

> **"**I'm not as hard on myself as I used to be. But that's what happens when you're growing up—you don't like things about yourself that much. I didn't like my body or my freckles or my red hair. I still don't like my freckles that much—they just bug me.**"**

City Music Hall's Rockettes, also worked as a Wall Street analyst and then became her daughter's manager. Lohan's younger brother, also named Michael, is an actor as well, having made his feature-film debut in a small role in *The Parent Trap*. Lohan has two other younger siblings, Aliana and Dakota.

With her striking red hair and green eyes, Lohan has been turning heads from an early age. She began modeling at age three, represented by the prestigious Ford Modeling Agency. She appeared in more than sixty television commercials during her childhood, advertising such brands as Pizza Hut, Wendy's, the Gap, and Jell-O. At age ten Lohan was cast as Alli Fowler on the soap opera *Another World,* a role she played from 1996 to 1997. In early 1997 the young actress learned that she had been chosen from a group of thousands of girls to star in a major film, Disney's remake of its 1961 classic *The Parent Trap*. Just as in the original, the role of the twin girls was played by a single actress, with Lohan doing the double duty first performed by Hayley Mills (1946–). Lohan successfully met the challenge of playing two different parts, skillfully portraying the girls' different personalities and even different accents. In the film, twin sisters Hallie and Annie are separated during their infancy when their parents divorce. Each grows up, one in the United States and the other in England, not knowing of the other's existence until they meet by chance at a summer camp. After initially clashing, the girls form a tight bond, and their newfound relationship leads to a master plan to reunite their mother and father.

Somewhat overwhelmed and tired out from her hard work in *The Parent Trap,* Lohan took a break from acting, resuming her "normal" life of going to school and spending time with friends. In 2000 she returned to show business, acting in *Life-Size,* a made-for-television Disney movie starring model and actress Tyra Banks. That same year Lohan was cast in a new sitcom, *Bette,* starring comedian, singer, and actress Bette Midler. But when the production for the show moved from New York to Los Angeles, Lohan chose to stay on the East Coast and left the show. Disney came calling again soon after, casting Lohan in *Get a Clue* (2002), a movie made for broadcast on the company's cable station, the Disney Channel.

Lindsay Lohan (right) and Jamie Lee Curtis at the premiere of **Freaky Friday.** Albert L. Ortega/ WireImage.com.

Drama queen rules comedies

Lohan's breakthrough role came in 2002, when she was cast as teenager Anna Coleman in another Disney remake, *Freaky Friday.* Lohan plays a teenage girl embroiled in constant conflict with her widowed mother, Tess Coleman, portrayed by Jamie Lee Curtis (1958–). Anna and Tess have little understanding of one another. Tess complains about her daughter's loud music, punk-rock clothing, and taste in boys. Anna resents her mother's plans to remarry, her attempts to control details of her daughter's life, and her refusal to take Anna's musical ambitions seriously. After dinner at a Chinese restaurant one night, Anna and Tess receive identical messages in their fortune cook-ies, a signal of the mysterious occurrence that results in mother and daughter waking up in each other's bodies the following morning. In a role originated in 1976 by acclaimed actress and director Jodie Foster (1962–), Lohan gracefully handled what amounts to a dual role: Anna the teenager and Tess the mother trapped in a teenager's body. The film, released in 2003, became a hit, its combination of wacky come-dy and touching family ties winning over adults as well as its younger target audience.

Her success in *Freaky Friday* launched Lohan to a new level of fame and made her a must-have actress for young-adult comedies. Lohan once again joined forces with Disney for *Confessions of a Teenage Drama Queen,* released in early 2004. The movie, about a drama-loving teenager coping with her family's move from the big city to the suburbs, earned lukewarm reviews, although many took note of Lohan's magnetic presence. She fared better in her next film, released a few months later. In *Mean Girls,* written by (and costar-ring) *Saturday Night Live* head writer Tina Fey, Lohan played Cady, a teen who grew up traveling the world with her scientist parents. Hav-ing been home-schooled all her life, Cady is unprepared for the viciously competitive world of high school cliques. With the help of some new friends, Cady takes on the school's most popular girls, a group known as the Plastics. *Mean Girls* charged ahead of its com-petitors at the box office, reaching number one in its first weekend of release. Michelle Tauber wrote in *People* magazine that this film marked a defining moment in Lohan's career: "Thanks to the critical and financial success of *Mean Girls* … Lohan has zipped straight to the head of the class."

Before her eighteenth birthday, Lohan had a number of success-ful, high-profile film roles under her belt, with more in the works, including yet another revisiting of a Disney classic (1968's *The Love Bug*) with *Herbie: Fully Loaded,* as well as the comedy *Dramarama.* Her visibility has meant that every step of her transition to adulthood has been documented by the media. Commenting on her physical development in her late teen years, some critics speculated that Lohan had surgery to increase her breast size, a rumor she denounced as ridiculous. A well-publicized tiff with fellow teen queen Hilary Duff revealed Lohan's tough, self-confident nature and, according to

Tauber in *People,* "established Lohan's reputation for making waves." Many news reports have suggested that Lohan heartily enjoys the nightlife, and she has been frequently spotted in clubs, dancing the night away with other young celebrities. Lohan has refused to apologize for her youthful behavior, telling *People* that "I'm 17. I'm learning, and I'd rather make my own mistakes and learn from them than have to be sheltered my whole life."

Not content to spend all of her time acting, Lohan has also begun developing a singing career. Crafting a style that combines pop, rock, and hip-hop, Lohan started working on her first album in 2003, having earlier signed a multi-album production deal with Emilio Estefan Jr. (1953–), a highly respected producer and the husband of singer Gloria Estefan (1957–). Lohan performed the song "Ultimate" for the soundtrack of *Freaky Friday,* helping the album reach *Billboard* magazine's top twenty. The young actress, filled with self-confidence, seems determined to explore her potential on a number of fronts. In numerous magazine articles, including a 2004 profile in *Girls' Life,* Lohan has explained the reasons behind her career choices and the decisions she makes in her personal life, by expresseing her go-for-it philosophy: "Life is way too short"—too short to worry about what other people think about her, too short to stay at home when she could be out dancing, and too short to settle for starring roles in films when she could become a pop star as well.

For More Information

Periodicals

Bryson, Jodi. "Confessions of a Teen Queen." *Girls' Life* (April-May 2004): p. 44.

Gostin, Nicki. "Newsmakers." *Newsweek* (February 23, 2004): p. 67.

Leydon, Joe. "*Freaky Friday.*" *Daily Variety* (July 21, 2003): p. 6.

"Lindsay Lohan." *People* (May 10, 2004): p. 26.

Tauber, Michelle. "Teen Star with a Twist." *People* (May 24, 2004): p. 79.

Web Sites

"Lindsay Lohan." *Internet Movie Database.* http://www.imdb.com/name/nm0517820/ (accessed on June 28, 2004).

"Lindsay's Biography." *LLRocks.com.* http://www.llrocks.com/index.php?a=bio.html&b=blank.html (accessed on June 28, 2004).

Stella McCartney

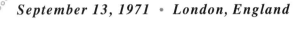

September 13, 1971 • London, England

Fashion designer

AP/Wide World Photos. Reproduced by permission.

While some may think that being the daughter of one of the world's most famous, respected, and wealthy rock stars would lead to plentiful advantages when building a career, British designer Stella McCartney might not completely agree. McCartney, daughter of Sir Paul—who happens to be a former member of the Beatles, perhaps the most popular and influential rock band ever—has talent and ambition to spare, but her fame-by-association has caused many to speculate that it is her family connections rather than her design collections that have propelled her career. Being a McCartney has its advantages—through family acquaintances, a teenaged Stella made important connections in the design world—but had she been lacking in talent and business sense, such connections would have been meaningless. Instead, McCartney proved that her combination of creativity, sense of style, and understanding of the fashion industry could make her a powerful force in fashion regardless of her parentage.

In 1997, less than two years after graduating from college, McCartney made headlines when she was hired as the creative director for Chloe, a respected design house in Paris, France. She spent four years at Chloe, helping to redefine the company's image and increasing the company's sales by appealing to young, hip consumers. In 2001 McCartney left Chloe to start her own company in partnership with the celebrated Gucci Group. She spent the following years issuing new collections, opening boutiques in New York, London, and Los Angeles, and, in 2003, launching a new fragrance line called Stella.

> "I have a vision for the way I want a woman to dress, perhaps because I'm a woman and know what I like to wear.... It's not about what it looks like in the studio or on the runway. It's what it looks like on a real person that matters."

Down on the farm

McCartney was born in London in 1971, not long after the breakup of the Beatles. Her father, a musician of exceptional talent, went on to form the band Wings, in which her mother, Linda, played keyboards and sang backup. Linda McCartney also became known for her skilled photographic portraits of musicians and other subjects, and was an outspoken advocate for animal rights as well as an accomplished vegetarian cook and cookbook writer. While the McCartneys led an unconventional life, traveling around the world on tour with the band with their children in tow, they were determined that their home base would be a tranquil refuge from the rock-and-roll lifestyle. The family, including Stella, her half-sister Heather (from Linda McCartney's first marriage), sister Mary, and brother James, moved to a farm by the time Stella was ten years old. Living in a modest farmhouse, the family raised sheep, rode horses, and grew organic produce. Stella was heavily influenced by the family's back-to-nature lifestyle and

Next-Generation Jagger

Jade Jagger, jewelry designer and famous offspring, has encountered much of the same skepticism that Stella McCartney has faced. As the daughter of Mick Jagger (1943–), lead singer of the Rolling Stones, and Bianca Jagger, a symbol of high fashion, Jade has struggled to establish an identity separate from that of her world-famous parents. Even as she has forged a successful design career, she still has critics suggesting that her professional accomplishments are due to her fame as a Jagger rather than her own talent.

Born in 1972, Jagger certainly had an unconventional upbringing as the daughter of one of rock music's most notorious bad boys. Her father has provided material for tabloid newspapers for most of his adult life, with one high-profile and stormy relationship after another (Mick and Bianca divorced around 1980). As a teenager Jade acquired a reputation for being a bit wild herself. She made headlines in 1988 when she was expelled from a prestigious private school in England for sneaking out to meet her boyfriend. And she was known for throwing, and attending, great parties. Jagger's lifestyle mellowed a bit when she became a mother in the early 1990s; she now has two daughters, Assisi and Amba.

Jagger has done some modeling and has long been a part of the fashion scene, but her vocation is designing jewelry. Jagger started her own company, Jade Inc., in 1998, creating and selling fine jewelry with a modern twist. In 2002 Jagger was hired as the creative director for the upscale British jewelry company Garrard. Once the Crown Jewelers—those responsible for crowns, tiaras, and other decorative items worn by British royalty—Garrard is a long-established traditional company that was formerly known as Asprey & Garrard. When those controlling the company split the brands into two separate firms, it was decided that Garrard, while remaining a provider of expensive luxury items, would also try to reach out to a younger and more informal crowd. Jagger was seen as the right person to navigate the company through this new territory.

In a 2002 article in *WWD,* Samantha Conti wrote that Jagger's goal at Garrard was to "blend the classic and the avant-garde, which means that blue diamond tiaras sell alongside funky gold dog tags, the rocks on some rings roll—literally—in a see-saw motion, and pendants are inspired by hip-hop and heraldry." Jagger designed a line of jewelry that playfully incorporated royal symbols such as crowns and family crests. While Jagger will never completely escape associations with her famous dad, she has forged a successful career independent of her family connections, earning praise for her funky and fashionable creations.

her parents' values, becoming a vegetarian herself as well as a committed animal rights activist.

McCartney had known ever since her early teen years that she wanted to be a fashion designer; she was designing and making clothes by age thirteen. At age fifteen she had a brief internship in Paris with acclaimed designer Christian LaCroix. Later, during her university years, McCartney became an apprentice to tailor Edward

Sexton, learning the finer points of tailoring on London's famed Savile Row, home to numerous traditional and highly respected custom clothing companies. She briefly worked at the French company Patou, makers of expensive custom-made clothes, but left the company in objection to their use of fur in some of their products.

McCartney attended Central Saint Martins College of Art and Design in London. Along with her fellow design students, McCartney designed a line of clothing to be displayed in a student fashion show as part of a graduation project. Like many of the other students, McCartney enlisted some friends to model her clothing during the show. Unlike her peers, however, McCartney's friends were supermodels Naomi Campbell and Kate Moss. Her models' fame, as well as her own celebrity stemming from her family ties (and the presence of her famous parents in the audience), attracted hordes of reporters and photographers from all over the world to the student show. Many of the other students resented the circus atmosphere and the fact that the press left the show immediately after McCartney's clothes had been shown. Some in the media and the fashion industry speculated that the extraordinary attention the young designer received had everything to do with her last name and little to do with her talent as a designer. But buyers for a number of upscale department stores, including Bergdorf Goodman and Neiman Marcus, disagreed, buying McCartney's line for sale in their stores.

A rapid rise

After her 1995 college graduation, McCartney opened her own boutique in London to sell her designs. Her designs featured a mix of crisp tailoring with lacy, romantic pieces, a combination that conveyed a sense of strong femininity. Her specialties were slip dresses and luxurious swishy silk skirts. "My mom always collected thrift-shop stuff—especially Italian slips," McCartney related to *Time* magazine's Ginia Bellafante. "I've always loved underwear and antique fabrics and lace for all their soft texture." Her designs were snapped up by fashion-conscious shoppers, including models, actresses, and musicians. In December of 1996, a man came into McCartney's boutique describing himself as the owner of a clothing store in Rome, Italy. He asked extensive questions about her collection and her ideas

Stella McCartney (center) acknowledges applause after a Paris fashion show in 2000. AP/Wide World Photos. Reproduced by permission.

on how to sell fashions to women of all ages, and was impressed by McCartney's thorough understanding of quality clothing as well as the marketing of such items. He later introduced himself as Mounir Moufarrige, president of the long-admired Parisian design firm Chloe. Moufarrige, eager to revive his struggling company by appealing to consumers younger and hipper than Chloe's traditional customers, had traveled to McCartney's shop to meet the woman who had been generating so much buzz.

Weeks later, Moufarrige offered the twenty-five-year-old designer a job as creative director of Chloe. Many in the fashion industry, including esteemed designer Karl Lagerfeld, who had previously held McCartney's position at Chloe, felt outraged that Moufarrige had hired a young and untested designer for such a significant position. McCartney soon silenced her critics, however, by bringing tremendous visibility and success to Chloe. Beginning with her first successful show with Chloe, in the fall of 1997, McCartney displayed her signature style of clean lines combined with delicate and sexy pieces. Critics acknowledged that her designs were not terribly bold or innovative, but they held tremendous appeal for consumers. McCartney not only improved the fortunes of Chloe, she also helped usher in a new trend in women's clothing that favored romantic, flirtatious styles over the plainer, no-frills look popular in the early 1990s. Just two years after she joined Chloe, Robin Givhan wrote in the *Washington Post* that under McCartney's direction, "Chloe has not just gotten substantially better. It has been transformed." McCartney's professional success, however, was tempered by personal tragedy during this period. In 1998 her mother died after a three-year battle with breast cancer.

In 2000 McCartney won the VH1/*Vogue* Fashion and Music Designer of the Year Award. During that same year, she designed a bridal gown for one of the most high-profile weddings in the celebrity world—that of pop superstar (and McCartney pal) Madonna to filmmaker Guy Ritchie. During 2001 McCartney led Chloe in a new direction, overseeing the introduction of a more casual, less expensive clothing line called See. Her success at Chloe and increasing name recognition as a designer to watch generated numerous rumors that McCartney would not stay at the Paris company much longer. Her rapid rise through the ranks of the fashion industry led many to believe that she would soon strike out on her own and, after four years with the Paris firm, McCartney did in fact leave. She had struck a deal with the renowned Gucci Group to start her own design house.

The ups and downs of independence

McCartney wasted no time creating the first line for her new company, which bears her name and is half owned by Gucci. Just a few months after striking out on her own in the fall of 2001, she showed her first collection. The reception was not exactly favorable. McCartney deviated from her signature style, as reported by Lisa Armstrong at *New York Metro.com:* "McCartney, who'd become a reliable source of lovely, easy-on-the-eye garments, chose this moment to replace her stock-in-trade flirtiness with something more hard-core." Armstrong pointed out that the timing of the show did not help matters; it took place one month after the terrorist attacks of September 11, 2001, in New York City and Washington, D.C., a time when people sought comfort, not confrontation. Fashion journalists wrote harsh reviews of the show, with McCartney's critics reiterating their opinion that the designer was famous simply because of her name. With her next few collections, however, McCartney once again proved her critics wrong. She returned to her roots, focusing on designing clothes that made women feel and look good.

In the fall of 2002 McCartney opened her first store, in New York City, to feature her new company's designs. Her second store opened the following spring in London, with a third opening in the Los Angeles area in the fall of 2003. In the stores, which are called simply "Stella McCartney," she sells her clothing as well as shoes, bags, and other accessories, including her own perfume, a scent called Stella. All of her products reflect McCartney's dedication to animal rights and other causes. In her clothing designs she emphasizes cottons and silks. Not one of her products, including shoes and bags, is made out of leather or fur. The company manufacturing her fragrance is prohibited from using genetically modified materials—that is, plants that have been altered by humans—and will not accept plants that were harvested by children or that are on any endangered species list. McCartney attributes her socially conscious attitude to the earthy styles of her parents, particularly her mother. She has also credited her mother with informing her fashion sensibility: the confidence to wear clothes she loves rather than following trends, a combination of vintage and modern looks, and the choice of a natural look over a highly polished one. Describing her mother's naturalness to Shane Watson of *Harper's Bazaar,* McCartney noted: "You look at people in her position now, and they're all manicured and their hair's straightened, and she was so not that, ever. She never waxed her legs, never dyed her hair, and that is so rare.… I mean, my mum really was the coolest chick in the world."

While the loss of her mother was devastating, McCartney has also experienced much personal and professional happiness in recent years. In August of 2003 she wed magazine publisher Alasdhair Willis in a small but elaborate ceremony. Taking place on a three-hundred-acre estate on the Scottish island of Bute, the wedding featured truckloads of white roses imported from the Netherlands, a bagpipe band,

and a fireworks display. Guests—including such celebrity pals as Gwyneth Paltrow, Liv Tyler, and Madonna—were transported in carriages pulled by Clydesdale horses. A large team of security guards kept the press at bay, ensuring a calm and private affair. On the professional front, McCartney has achieved increasing success with each new collection. Tom Ford, the former creative director of Gucci, told Armstrong why he has so much confidence in McCartney: "She has everything it takes to be successful—the drive, the will, and the intelligence. She has great style, great taste."

For More Information

Periodicals

"And I Love Her." *People* (September 15, 2003): p. 66.

Bellafante, Ginia. "Tired of Chic Simple? Welcome to the New Romance." *Time* (April 6, 1998): p. 66.

Conti, Samantha. "Jagger's New Jewels." *WWD* (September 16, 2002): p. 17.

Diamond, Kerry. "Stella's Sexy New Scent." *Harper's Bazaar* (September 2003): p. 248.

Fallon, James. "Life with Gucci." *WWD* (July 3, 2001): p. 1.

Givhan, Robin. *Washington Post* (January 29, 1999): p. C1.

Watson, Shane. "Twenty-four Hours with Stella McCartney." *Harper's Bazaar* (September 2002): p. 426.

Web Sites

Armstrong, Lisa. "Stella Nova." *New York Metro.com.* http://www.newyork metro.com/shopping/articles/02/fallfashion/stellanova/ (accessed on July 14, 2004).

Stella McCartney. http://www.stellamccartney.com/ (accessed on July 14, 2004).

"Who's Who: Stella McCartney." *Vogue.com.* http://www.vogue.co.uk/ whos_who/Stella_McCartney/default.html# (accessed on July 14, 2004).

Volume numbers are in italic; **boldface** *indicates main entries and their page numbers; (ill.) following a page number indicates an illustration on the page.*

C

h

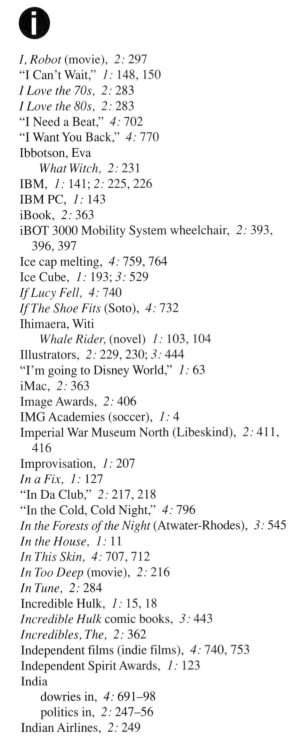

n

◉

X